Somebody Else's Century

Somebody Else's Century

EAST AND WEST IN A
POST-WESTERN WORLD

Patrick Smith

PANTHEON BOOKS, NEW YORK

Grateful acknowledgment is made to the following for permission
to reprint previously published material:
Donald Richie: Excerpt from Donald Richie's conversation with Yukio Mishima
from *The Japan Journals, 1947–2004*, edited by Leza Lowitz (Berkeley: Stone
Bridge Press, 2005). Reprinted by permission of Donald Richie.

University of California Press: Poem by Basho from *Religion and Nothingness* by
Keiji Nishitani, translated by Jan van Bragt, copyright © 1982 by Keiji Nishitani.
Reprinted by permission of the University of California Press.

Certain passages originally appeared in different form in *Asian Art News*,
the Bloomberg news wire, the *International Herald Tribune*, *The New Yorker*,
and *The Washington Quarterly*.

Library of Congress Cataloging-in-Publication Data

Smith, Patrick (Patrick L.)
Somebody else's century : east and west in a post-western world / Patrick Smith.
p. cm.
Includes bibliographical references.
ISBN 978-0-375-42550-9
1. East and West. 2. Japan—Civilization—Western influences. 3. National
characteristics, Japanese. 4. Social change—Japan. 5. China—Civilization—
Western influences. 6. National characteristics, Chinese.
7. Social change—China. 8. India—Civilization—Western influences.
9. National characteristics, East Indian. 10. Social change—India. I. Title.
CB251.S63 2010 950—dc22 2009043556

www.pantheonbooks.com

Printed in the United States of America
First Edition
2 4 6 8 9 7 5 3 1

This book is for R. H. S.,
ever and very there

It is to the memory of Ryszard Kapuściński,
a friend in life, a dear friend by way of all the work

History is marked by alternating movements across an imaginary line that separates East from West . . .

—HERODOTUS, *The Histories*

Contents

A Note on Names

Japanese and Chinese make various choices when naming themselves in international company, and I have sought in this book to respect individual preferences. I have not, then, imposed a standard form. Sometimes the family name is first, sometimes the given name, and the context or the second mention should make clear which.

Another such judgment concerned Indian cities. One hears "Bombay" and one hears "Mumbai," "Calcutta" and "Kolkata." I have settled on the names used during the British era and the first decades after independence, the thought being that they will be more familiar to some readers, and a layer of history might just as well be left intact.

Somebody Else's Century

Introduction

"But surely," I said, "the real Japan must still exist some-
place or other if you look around for it."

He shook his head.

"Is there no way to save it?" I wondered.

"No," he said, "there is nothing left to save."

—DONALD RICHIE, in conversation with

Yukio Mishima (1970)

SOME SUMMERS AGO, during a time I kept an apartment in central Tokyo, two friends from Boston wrote to say they would come for a visit. An attorney and a designer, they were new to Asia, past and present. It was their first journey across the Pacific, Japan their first stop on a tour of the region.

After several days' wandering along Tokyo's broad avenues and through the narrow, hidden lanes behind them, the time had come, these two said, to see something of Japan. Tokyo, after all, was not Japan: It was a modern city. (And in truth it is not Japan, if we mean as Paris is not France and New York not America.) So we settled on a route, got the car out, and drove southwest into the green of rice paddies and tea terraces and then into the high, forested mountains beyond them.

Lunchtime approached. At the edge of a village, and with a clear, stony stream behind it, I spotted a place I thought would do. It served *tonkatsu*, deep-fried pork. For some reason, many *tonkatsu* restaurants tend to serve only *tonkatsu*, and so it was that day in Yamanashi Prefecture. It is not the most desirable summer dish, *tonkatsu*, but it has a history. The Japanese came up with it in the late nineteenth century, when they were absorbing Western ways and inventing their version of European cuisine. It is an orphan of a certain time, then. I related some of this as we ordered our *biru* (which, of course, the Japanese learned from the Germans to brew).

My friends seemed a touch disappointed to hear the tale of *tonkatsu*.

"But is this a real Japanese way of eating?" one asked. It was the attorney.

Their eyes began to wander. There was a window in the front, and in it a few of those plastic models the Japanese use to display the dishes on offer—in this case *tonkatsu* this way, that way, or the other way. An extension cord ran out the back to a light near the stream. There were fluorescent tubes—the circular kind, with dangling string—and a refrigerator with a glass door, behind which stood all the brown bottles of *biru:* Asahi, Sapporo, Kirin. When lunch came, the *patron* asked politely if we would prefer knives and forks to chopsticks.

"Is this a real Japanese restaurant?" my lawyer friend persisted.

I HAD FORGOTTEN THIS INCIDENT—why recall it?—until many years and miles later when I was passing through Calicut. Calicut lies along the southern end of the Malabar Coast, the Indian edge of the Indian Ocean. It stares westward, and it is where da Gama landed in 1498. I had my heart set on seeing the very spot where, I imagined, a pair of heavy leather boots sank into the sand half a millennium earlier and the modern encounter between East and West can be said to have begun.

In town I looked up a professor named John Ochanthuruth. John had taught history and knew the terrain thoroughly. By way of maps, texts, diaries, documents, and years of exploring the coastline, he could tell you precisely when and where da Gama dropped anchor (the evening of May 20 at a place called Kappad, where there is a monument), when and where the Portuguese came ashore (the next day, at a nearby village called Pandarani), and the route the thick-thighed explorer took to meet the *zamorin*, ruler of the Calicut kingdom.

On the way to the coastline, John wanted me to see some things. He took me to the pepper market that had made Calicut a center of global trade centuries before the Portuguese came.

He showed me fourteenth-century mosques built like Hindu temples and mosques with Greek columns and arches. We passed Hindu temples that resembled roadside Christian chapels. We talked about matrilineal Muslims and the ancient Jews and Syrian Christians who had settled in southern India. We talked about the Parsi cemetery, inscriptions around town chiseled in Arabic, and all the Portuguese words embedded in Malayalam, the local language.

A narrative thread emerged. Hindus, Arabs, Persians, Turks, Nestorians, Alexandrians, Abyssinians, Venetians, a few Chinese, a few Javanese—they had all come and made of Calicut and the Malabar Coast the scene of a glorious syncretism. Da Gama, as Indians do not tire of telling you, had discovered nothing: He had sailed into a world that was already churning. It was an Arab pilot he had picked up on the East African coast who had read the winds for him and had guided him along the route he took.

The stout, graceless Portuguese did transform this bazaar of humanity, however. Refused a trading monopoly, da Gama had his guns blazing by 1503. Within a few years many spice merchants had fled for what would now be called the United Arab Emirates. What had been an all-welcome sort of place was soon a matter of blood and gore, divide and conquer, and local enmities previously unthought of. The jihad Calicut's Muslims later declared may count as the first in the modern era. The West had come eastward—in a certain way hauling the Crusades into the modern age.

Da Gama's monument turned out to be a miserable little block of mildewed concrete, an obelisk not much taller than a beach umbrella. It had a tiny plaque embedded in it and was surrounded by a broken fence and a considerable amount of litter. And between the monument and the shoreline, something interesting: The villagers had erected a small mosque. It was bleached pale green by the sun and had a corrugated roof with two truncated minarets; by all appearances it was not much used. The point seemed to lie in the semiology: There would be a Muslim place of worship between the Portuguese sailor's plaque and the sea that had carried him here.

Walking the shoreline, John told me a curious tale. Some years earlier, as the five-hundredth anniversary of da Gama's landing approached, scholars planned to mark the occasion. Researchers would gather; papers would be presented. A replica of da Gama's ship was to sail the original route. New Delhi would support the proceedings, along with various Portuguese foundations. Then the shoe dropped in the villages and at the Malabar Christian College, proposed host of what had grown into an assortment of events. No, there would be no commemorating the coming of those colonizing Europeans. There would be no seminars, no ship, and certainly no money from New Delhi. Protesters came from as far as Goa, a day's travel northward. And all came to nothing: There was not a single event to mark da Gama's landfall.

"In the end," John said with a rueful smile, "they came to the monument and threw dung all over it."

He paused, a little lost in the events he had just recounted. We were between the empty, silent mosque and the sand, which was by then too hot to walk upon.

"The idea was not to celebrate anything," John said after a while. "It was to analyze, to understand. We wanted to try to remember."

"Remember what, John?"

"To remember ourselves."

WHAT DOES THE GREEN of summer in Yamanashi-*ken* have to do with the sandy land of southern India? Why think of a long-ago lunch in the Japanese countryside while sitting on fallen palm fronds along the Malabar Coast?

It has to do with perspective—which, bringing it to a single word, is the subject of this book. These essays are about seeing—or just as much its opposite, which is not precisely blindness so much as a failure to overcome received assumptions (or to know, even, that one has received them and lives by them). Clouded vision is merely a symptom of the malady, not the malady itself. The malady is lodged in our minds.

Japan, the "real" Japan one arrives from the West in search of, does not have extension cords running along its floors. Japan is made of wood and thatch and *shimenawa*, that textured twine hung in Shinto shrines, and of course of silk, translucent rice paper, and bamboo. It is not made of glass and steel and plastic in artificial colors. If it is modern it cannot be Japanese, and we cannot have found what we came to seek, for if it is modern it must be Western. Above all, it does not have Westerners walking around in it: We, having arrived, must feel as if we have transcended our own world and entered another, where only "others" dwell. The sensation of entering is important precisely because we desire the sensation of exiting.

My Boston friends reflected this, though hardly could they have known it. The incident in Calicut was another matter. That was a case of conscious subtraction. We Asians were over here, all together and doing fine, and then the Westerners came, and Asia ceased to be Asia. Instead, it became something spoiled, something derailed, something not itself. The endeavor is to overcome this despoliation—in a word, to resume. There are many versions of this narrative, depending on where one is, all sounding the same thematic notes: harmony, intrusion, one or another combination of nostalgia and what the French call *ressentiment*, and some inchoate desire to find what was lost and begin again.

The clearest expression of this story line I have ever heard, shorn of all extraneous detail, was delivered during an evening at a private club in Hong Kong. My host was named Paul Ho, the grandson of a noted nineteenth-century reformer, a prolific presence on the late-Qing political scene called Kang Youwei. I was about to make an extended trip into the Chinese countryside, and Ho wanted to introduce a friend who had spent most of his life on the mainland. "He has a certain perspective," Ho explained.

Dinner proceeded, the dishes came and went, and so did the conversation with the same variety. We talked about Chinese ideograms and yin and yang, the New Culture Movement of the 1920s and Mao. My friend's friend, an older man with gray stubble and a brittle physique, was named Joe Poon. At one point I asked him about the various kinds of nostalgia I find during travels in China. These fascinate me: There is Shanghai nostalgia, Xi'an nostalgia, Beijing nostalgia, Suzhou nostalgia, nostalgia for the 1920s, the 1950s, the nineteenth century; nostalgia for Ming, nostalgia for Sung. Each version has implicitly within it an idea of how China should be and a critique of how it is. Nostalgia is a subject threaded through these essays, as it is a characteristic sentiment among many Asians—if not, indeed, most of them.

"Not too much," Joe Poon replied. "I don't see too much of it."

He thought for a moment. And then: "There's sentimental nostalgia, which means the past was better than the present. Then there's rational nostalgia, logical nostalgia, which means the past was logically better than the present."

"You've switched but a single word," I protested.

At this, Joe Poon piped up. We were headed into what the Japanese would call the *honne*, the inner truth, of his thinking.

"Let me tell you about village life in China," Joe Poon began. "You know about the old villages?"

"Well, as a matter—"

"Let me tell you.

"In the Chinese village, there was a mulberry tree. That's first. Then in the mulberry tree there were silkworms. The silkworms used to drop their droppings into a lake next to the tree. The fish ate the droppings. Then the droppings of the fish settled at the bottom. And then we scooped up the droppings of the fish from the lake and . . . How do you say? In the fields . . ."

"Fertilized."

"Fertilized the fields with the fish droppings. You can't use human waste unless it is . . . They do something to it first."

"Processed."

"Processed. So it was an environmental circle. The water was always sweet, the air clean, we had clothes, we had food, there were no divisions of anything within the village. It was a society of conservation, not of consumption. You had the man, the spouse, the household; there was no divorce."

Joe Poon skipped half a beat and then continued.

"But the Western people came along and introduced what?"

At this, Joe Poon banged his fist on the table—escalating things, I considered, beyond any point of retrieval. I offered no answer.

"Opium," Joe Poon exclaimed. "Pollution. Consumption."

There was another pause. Then: "I don't hate foreigners. I'm just telling you history as if—how do you say?—looking down from the stars."

Joe Poon seemed to have found a resting place. Our host alternated between glances at me and a search for something in the middle distance he might plausibly stare at for a while.

"Interesting," I said, and indeed it was. The imagery reminded me of the paintings one sometimes finds on old fans and scrolls. This was Chinese nostalgia and *ressentiment*, that term we will consider later, in its purest form. China had once been whole and untarnished and its people contented. Then came the West, and all was disrupted.

EVERYONE, WESTERNER OR EASTERNER, has his or her Asia. My companions from Boston had theirs, and the vague disappointment that overtook them as they began their travels is standard among first-time arrivals. Joe Poon, emphatically enough, had an Asia: Even if he gave an account "from the stars"—a big-picture account, a bird's-eye view—he considered it accurate. The Muslims of Calicut had an Asia of their own devising, as did Donald Richie and Mishima. The Chinese, the Japanese, the Indians, all of the societies surrounding these, and then certainly Westerners—we all have our Asias. No place else, not even contentious America, seems to inspire so many ideas as to what it is.

One may work through numerous of these notions. In the course of some years as a correspondent, I have concocted a term intended to counter all our inadequate perspectives (wrong; yes and no; sort of true, sort of not; yes but misleading, and so on). Awkward but to me irreducible, it is written here and there in many notebooks as "AAII," or, if I was in a scientific mood, "A^2I^2." It means simply "Asia as it is," and it describes a way of seeing—the seeing of things past conventions and commonly held assumptions.

This term is not intended to take on any life of its own beyond its occasional use in these essays. It is not coined to keep pace with the inventions of clever newspaper columnists. It has a use. This comes to an act of subtraction in some cases and in others one of addition. It is meant to suggest that Asia can be modern and still be Asia. It is meant to discourage useless habits: dropping the modern era as somehow not part of the Asian story, assuming that "Asia" ended when East and West encountered each other and all that followed must somehow be erased. To put this another way, the West is indelibly part of the East—now and as it has been throughout the modern era. This cancels all searches for an uncontaminated Asia, for such a thing cannot be retrieved.

If we are to see Asia as it is, nothing is to be censored—and certainly not blocked out in the manner of, say, the Chinese authorities today. We do not avert our eyes or imagine: A building in Osaka or Madras that looks as if it could stand in Kansas City is a Japanese or an Indian building. We do not paint rural idylls on paper fans (as Joe Poon did), or paint ourselves out of the picture (as my Boston friends did), or move the picture's frame to exclude part of the canvas (as Calicut's Muslims did). Above all, we neither mourn nor regret, as my friend Donald Richie did, for there is no more (or less) to mourn or regret in Asia than there is anywhere else. Nor do we think in terms of "nothing left to save." Mishima was his own Orientalist on his own search for the exotic. It is indefensible, but the great novelist meant it: He took his own life shortly after the conversation Richie recorded in *The Japan Journals*—we must assume because he believed somewhere within himself that a Japanese life in 1970 was not worth saving.

If it helps give us perspective, we can think in terms of background and foreground. There is the remote past and the recent, and they are both parts of the picture. Above all, we—we Westerners in this case—must dispense with any illusions that we are not within the frame, moving around in the story. Our engagement with the East has been intimate for a century and a half; the foreground has its own history now. There is nothing left in Asia to "come upon" that does not already involve us. There is a strong but useful term to name this condition. Asia is miscegenated, the first portion of the planet that can be so described. To grasp this is to grasp Asia as it is.

BY WAY OF RICHNESS and variety, it seems to me, all pasts are equal—logically enough and no surprise, since our pasts are one in the end (or at their beginning). If we consider continuity, however, East and West are different. The history of the East is as filled with great events as anyplace else, but Asia does not think in terms of departures. The past is not "another country." Nothing of it is left behind, however sharp a turn in the road may be. Past and present are indivisible, and events are understood to lie in a long line. The remote past is not so remote as we Westerners assume because of the way we imagine our own past has unrolled—momentously, discontinuously, often abruptly. "It's history" cannot have in Asia the dismissive ring it has for Americans.

Asia took on Western habits in matters of chronology during the modern era. But they were superimposed, and the old notion of time's flow and fluidity has always remained beneath the surface. The past is still the way one understands, and sometimes defines and determines, the present. It is now generally accepted that Mao, who condemned the Confucian classics before the great, broad masses, spent evenings reading them for guidance as to how a proper ruler rules. Ask an Indian about the religious strife in Gujarat, the Indian state where South and West Asia have touched and mingled for millennia, and you are likely to get back an account of things that begins with a Hindu temple that was sacked in 1026, or with a sixteenth-century mosque in the north of India that was burned in 1992 because, the arsonists believed, there had been a temple there before it. This is "social memory," and it is made more powerful in Asia precisely because so much that is modern has been placed atop it.

Animosities between Hindus and Muslims notwithstanding, among the notable attributes of the continuous Asian past is how inclusive and absorptive it has tended to be. In this the *zamorin's* domain in Calicut was nothing exceptional. Da Gama, by contemporary accounts, was welcomed with extravagant ceremony when the sailor's entourage, passing through throngs of cheering onlookers, reached the royal court. It was eight days after those heavy boots hit the sand, and already da Gama was part of Asia—Asia as it is (or was then). He was hardly the first Westerner to set foot in the East, but, yes, something new entered the frame when he did. At that moment there was a very considerable departure. This had to do with da Gama's choices, how he determined to manage things, which in turn reflected material advances Asia had not yet made. Nothing more. And beneath the commotion, things fundamental remained as they were.

Asia as it is, then: To be part of it has nothing to do with skin color, the shape of one's eyes, shophouses, strong family ties—and still less with anything so modern as national frontiers, which do not come naturally to Asians and often sit awkwardly upon their lands and seas. Nothing so fixed comes into it. Better to think of a large part of the planet in constant flux, a part that is by definition without definition: The "as it is" is always changing. Fixedness, our new century will require us to recognize, is a Western trope.

China—in many minds (including Chinese minds) that most fixed and homogeneous of domains—is worth a moment's consideration. Ai Weiwei, the noted artist, once began a conversation with the observation that if we are going to think about China, we need to decide which one we mean. Han China (which was in fact rather small)? Tang China (which extended far out west)? Manchu China (the China of the Qing, which collapsed in 1911)? They were all different. None of what is now "southern China" was China until nearly 1700, not quite a century and a half after Francis Xavier made landfall (and then died) in Shangchuan, a part of not-yet-China. The China we mean when we say "China" today, with its reluctant Tibetans and Uighurs, is but a half century old. It is *a* China. The in-built myopia of the living: We—we, all of us—will have to overcome it if we are to understand and situate ourselves.

"It is plural, it is fragmented, it is disrupted. Some of its 'traditions' died a long time ago. Others have persisted in 'mediated' form, in Western and Eastern minds alike."

I was in a conversation with a retired Harvard professor named Lee Ou-fan, we were both living in Hong Kong, and our subject was China. But all Lee said can as well apply to all of Asia, and I do not doubt he would accept this as so.

There is plenty of background and foreground in the professor's account. This is natural: To distinguish between the two is the way we look at and understand pictures. But the distinction is in our minds, not on any canvas, and so it is with Asia. In the end, there is not so much difference as we might think between what lies deep in the past and what lies just behind us or before us. The inclusiveness of Asia's past—the Syrian Christians, the Venetians, and all the others on our list—is not much different from the inclusiveness of the present (which includes us Westerners). So we can make use of the aesthetic habit of seeing background and foreground, but then we must put it aside for the sake of seeing the whole.

PART OF WHAT IT MEANS to be Chinese today is to be confused about what it means to be Chinese. I know of no Chinese alive who does not, in some fashion, entertain this question. Equally, to be Japanese in the twenty-first century means to have considered and put aside, one way or another, some of one's "Japaneseness." Indians, maybe more than any other people, are confident of themselves and of what it means to be Indian. Nonetheless, to be Indian now is to suffer a certain anxiety as to the fragility of one's Indianness. I did not begin with these observations. They were not in my notebooks so that I might go in search of confirmation. They are where I ended up.

Why this widespread ambiguity, from the Bosporus to Tokyo Bay? True enough, people the world over put such questions to themselves. Brazilians and Nigerians do; Americans certainly do. In Europe the line of inquiry is a matter of public debate. (What does it mean nowadays to be French?) Nowhere but Asia, however, does the question plunge so deeply into the psyche. In Europe and America, "What does it mean . . . ?" questions are generally matters of skin color and birth certificates—and veils (an odd obsession, truly, given Christians invented them as tokens of observance). In Asia, it is different: Who am I? If I say "Chinese," what do I mean? What makes me Chinese? If I say "Asian"—and not all Asians, notably Indians, care for the term—what does that mean?

Why is this? Why would more than half of humanity be so engaged in so fundamental a point of self-understanding?

In a similar vein, I have had few encounters with Asians, or witnessed many between Asians and Westerners, that did not bear the burden, however faintly, of 150 years of history and an attendant question of equality and inequality. Maybe it is a matter of having overcome this complication in one relationship or another—or perhaps in many. But then lingers the consciousness of overcoming. One way or another, there seems no escape—at least not for us, we with a foot in the last century.

Many friends—Western friends, never Asians—find this thought shocking. How egregiously Western of you, they may as well exclaim. How deeply Orientalist. I fail to see any reason for this. These are frequently the same people to explain the place of hierarchy in Asian relationships—the "above" and "below" of them. To the extent Asians understand others by way of rank, should Westerners consider themselves exempt? We are exceptions somehow—painted out of the picture? To indulge in a little immanent critique, how hopelessly Orientalist. We must learn to "think with history," as an American writer has put it. Shocking it would be if, given all that has happened between East and West in the modern era, the past were not present in our encounters.

It should not be too difficult to see deeply enough into our cross-cultural intimacies to discover some of what lies beneath them. Close, casual, glancing—a friend, a colleague, a cabdriver—there are always things to find, and I now note three because they are to be taken up in these essays.

One is nostalgia, and I have already mentioned it. I have long considered nostalgia a form of depression. Whatever else it is made of, nostalgia implies a certain inaccurate relationship with the past and a defense against the present—the past as refuge. If nostalgia has been so prevalent among Asians for so long, we must ask why.

I have mentioned *ressentiment*, too, and this bears brief elaboration. I would like to remain with the French term because it means something more than our "resentment." It implies a submerged sensation of impotence (and we can take this word in its fullest meaning) in the face of another. It is a consuming emotion, difficult to escape, as there is a constant return to it and to the animosity it provokes. It involves, finally, the ennobling of the supposedly inferior and a devaluing of the supposedly superior. Joe Poon, to take a ready example, was a brimming chalice of *ressentiment*. It also involves groups and societies (as in nations), not only individuals. It was the Germans who first borrowed the term and elaborated its meaning: They had no word to match it. Max Scheler, one of the great thinkers of the last century, explored the phenomenon exhaustively, and anyone familiar with his work will recognize the way it is used in this one.

Finally, there is the matter of weakness—the sensation of it and the fact of it. To take this as the reality of weakness in the face of superior power is to understand the phenomenon only in part. Asia's sensation of weakness has run far more deeply in the modern era. The West's manifest material superiority led Asians to conclude they were possessed of a defective inheritance. There arose from this an impulse to surrender to a fundamental assumption of inadequacy: This is what we mean by weakness.

Here are a few lines from two Matthew Arnold poems, both published in 1867. The "younger world" in the first refers to the West:

The brooding East with awe beheld
Her impious younger world;

The Roman tempest swell'd and swell'd,
And on her head was hurl'd.

The East bow'd low before the blast,
In patient, deep disdain.
She let the legions thunder past,
And plunged in thought again.

—"Obermann Once More"

And this:

Ah! Now 'tis changed. In conquering sunshine bright
The man of the bold West now comes array'd;
He of the mystic East is touch'd with night.

—"East and West"

Arnold was a man of his time—there is no arguing this. These lines describe, among other things, what the East's weakness looked like to a Victorian Englishman midway through the era of conquest and colonization. They are a kind of anatomy lesson. "Brooding," "patient," "deep," "plunged in thought," "mystic": This was the Asian, scarcely a match for those impious legions (well-chosen word) of bold Westerners with all that sunshine on them. Arnold at least seemed to allow as to the East's contributions to the West's material superiority, so implying the seesaw of world history. But we can improve on the thought, surely.

Nehru, in *The Discovery of India*, took particular issue with the matter of thundering armies galloping past indolent locals. Not an apt description of India or what happened, he asserted. "Always she has resisted them, sometimes successfully, sometimes unsuccessfully," Nehru wrote, "and even when she failed for the time being, she has remembered and prepared herself for the next attempt." True enough, setting aside India's remarkable capacity to absorb everything that comes at it and then making it its own. And we now know, by way of India's

"subaltern" school and its scholarship-from-the-bottom fol-
lowers elsewhere, that resistance has been a fact of life all
along and everywhere in the modern encounter between East
and West.

But we cannot throw all of nineteenth-century Europe's perspective overboard. It would be, as an Indian friend once put
it, "a cheap victory in any case." *Fukoku kyohei,* "rich nation,
strong army," was one of the prominent slogans of Meiji Japan,
and it tells us two things the Japanese found they were not
after Westerners began to come. In China the discourse
from the mid-nineteenth century onward had to do with "self-
strengthening," and it is the same: We understand by way
of a mirror. China-as-victim has become so ingrained in the
national psyche since the Opium Wars that one might easily
despair of mainlanders ever getting beyond it, however powerful they make themselves. In the case of India we have no
need of mirrors. There is an extensive literature since the
late nineteenth century having to do with weakness: We are
weak; our character is innately weak; we are physically weak;
the Hindu has weakened over centuries of decline. Many
were the Indian writers, thinkers, and zealots who began to
take up these themes at roughly the same time Arnold wrote his
lines.

CONFUSION AND ANXIETY; nostalgia, *ressentiment,* weakness: It
is perhaps plain that in looking at Asia I see no use in treating
these things delicately. The habit of tiptoeing has made no
small contribution to many large misunderstandings, usually
flowing in an easterly direction. I would see no use in taking up
these matters at all had they not risen so manifestly close to the
surface since I arrived in Asia nearly three decades ago. There
is nothing new about them; they have been newly evident, and
now at last they are beginning to disappear. In their place we
can detect a nascent self-possession the East has not known for

many centuries. This is what is new among Asians—elusive, unannounced, and unmistakable all at once. And it was to capture something of so fundamental a change that these essays were conceived and written.

Among the reactions of Easterners to the coming of Westerners centuries ago was the habit of occlusion. One can sense it in some of the old texts and see it in the old paintings. To occlude was nothing Asians did not do among themselves. The Japanese have terms for it: There was the *honne* of something, the inner truth of it, and the *tatemae*, the published, articulated version. The elaborate filigree in an Islamic palace window is there so that one can see out without being seen. But between East and West this habit has lasted a long time. And it has seemed to me that part of what has been occluded is a vast lake of grief, within which much is suspended. This lake is now evaporating, leaving all that lives in it plain for us to see, even as those suspended things are destined not to survive.

The ebbing of nostalgia and *ressentiment*, the arrival of a certain clarity as to one's identity and place in history—this is what is new when one looks at Asia today. It marks a fundamental turn in our world. It is another of those departures that will leave much undisturbed but, at the same time, bring much change. It is the newness of this turn in thinking and feeling and seeing, not the old emotions and habits, that is the subject of the essays that follow.

WHAT WE HAVE commonly called the Asian challenge has preoccupied the West for many years. We have meant, invariably, a material challenge and an attendant accumulation of power. Since the 1980s a challenge of this kind has come, indeed, to mesmerize us. Late in that decade the scholar Paul Kennedy gave us his famous thesis: Powers rise and decline in a westerly direction, first across the Atlantic and in our time across the Pacific. To me this has always seemed beyond question, providing one recognized where we stood in history. When Boutros Boutros-Ghali, the UN's controversial secretary-general, stepped down in 1996 and later wrote his memoirs, I agreed with him exuberantly. "Single-superpower hegemony is a transitory phenomenon," he concluded. But for years one had to argue the point. Now America's pattern—its destiny, we may say—is manifest. The "benevolent hegemon" (an astonishing oxymoron invented in the late 1990s) cannot even count its days because there are none left. This is the undulation of history. Nobody announces rises and declines, Kennedy might have noted for us: They happen before our eyes but often in the manner of the undressed emperor until they are hard upon us.

These essays are intended to move in more closely than history's long waves, to something nearer to its *longue durée*—the things that endure however certain we are that we have left them behind. What distinguishes Asia in our time is the completion or near completion of the very project—an essentially material project—that has defined it the whole of the modern era. Now a project of another kind has begun. It is the source of the true Asian challenge, and we have so far failed to register it.

It is useful to think of a construction site. Modernizing in Asia has meant above all the making of a new material world and the erection of institutions identified as parts of the apparatus of the modern: skyscrapers, rail systems, telephone networks; parliaments, judiciaries, ballot boxes, tax regimes. Japan, ever first among Asians, is finished in this respect: The job is done. For others the end is in sight. But we come to another of the paradoxes that speckle these essays. It is the completion of the one construction project that prompts another that is far more profound. Here we will borrow from Rabindranath Tagore, India's first Nobelist. There is "modernization" and there is "becoming modern." The latter concerns the construction of a modern self, the rebuilding of what Japanese feminists once taught me to call "the edifice within." This is what we Westerners witness but miss in the new century's Asia. And the impulse in this direction is immensely powerful. All the ripping down of the old and throwing up of the new across China today cannot be explained as a matter of economic necessity alone. It is too frantic to be considered so simply. The visible Chinese project is, among much else, a signifier of an almost compulsive psychological urge to self-reinvent—to make "being Chinese" mean something new.

FOR THOSE OF THE EAST, among the most fundamental experiences of the modern era has been a phenomenon scholars call doubling. Various Asian writers and thinkers have identified this practice since the late nineteenth century. Doubling is in part a reflection of the habit of occlusion noted earlier. With the arrival of the modern, the Asian self tended to divide into two: There was a traditional self and a modern self. The former wore kimono or robes or a sarong, belonged to a family, clan, or village in the established way, and situated himself or herself in life as part of a continuous flow. The modern self was very different; it was something one "put on." The modern self wore stiff collars and leather shoes, moved among strangers, and was taxed to live as an ego-centered individual without all the old psychological fortifications. These two selves lived side by side, the one partly occluding the other. It is not too much to suggest that together they constituted the modern Asian personality. In each individual there was a reference to an "other."

The doubled self lent Asians certain attributes. The modern self was given to absorption without resistance. All things and habits Western were to be accepted, learned, and incorporated. Scientific thinking, manners, a preoccupation with facts as against understanding, the Western notion of time: The modern self took on all such things. The traditional self was given

to occlusion by way of protection and withdrawal. The inva-
lidity of the un-modern, the familiar, the indigenous: This
became a preoccupation. A paradox formed. What was local
and traditional was inferior, but it was also treasured. It was a
question of the authentic and the inauthentic: The doubled self
may live one way but was genuinely something else. And it was
on this paradox that sensations of weakness, impulses toward
the nostalgic, and one degree or another of *ressentiment* were
suspended.

Westerners have no experience of doubling in this way. We
will have difficulty, then, understanding the phenomenon, then
why the phenomenon is coming to an end, and finally why this
is of fundamental importance. After 150 years with the modern, the modern has lost its strangeness for Asians. Neither is
the modern understood any longer to be Western. Asia has
arrived at this point, ironically, precisely because it put on the
West, as Nietzsche wrote of it, for so long. So does it come to
a renewed self-possession, a recovered idea of itself relative
to the West. The need for doubling as a psychological habit
fades, because the traditional and the modern, the Eastern and
the Western, the indigenous and the imported are all valid aspects of a twenty-first-century consciousness. To put the point
plainly, the West's monopoly on the modern is now behind us.
This is a change of epochal consequence.

There are contradictions, more apparent than real. China is
Westernizing beyond anything the most Western of Westerners might have imagined. How can this be said to reflect the
throwing off of a world and the old, humiliated self that
dwelled in it? Such knots need to be untied. In China's case we
need to recognize Westernization as method, not intent—
means, not end. It is one stage leading to others; the story is not
yet finished. "Become who you are," Nietzsche famously urged
us. I have always considered it to be the fortunate few who are
able to follow this advice. Asians are not few, and many are in

no wise fortunate. But their great act of becoming can scarcely be missed when one is among them.

THIS IS NOT a useful book in the way we ordinarily think of one. We will not evaluate the GDP statistics of China, India, or any other country mentioned. We will not think overmuch about cars, currencies, production platforms, or comparative advantage in this or that industry. We are not interested in manufacturing versus services versus high-technology research. The neglect of these topics is altogether by design.

We in the West have an odd way of looking eastward. It is odd because it is at the very latest a late-nineteenth-century way of seeing. At the time, the more clear-eyed among us—Twain, a few others—explained that our point of view was that of an exploiting people looking across to and down on those exploited. We were utilitarians, and Asia had a use. Today we can fairly describe our perspective as in essence technocratic. It is "economy centered" and grounded in instrumental rationality. This is because our discourse on Asia is shaped primarily by business executives and policy planners—two not-unrelated kinds of people. With notable exceptions, the press and the broadcasters have played their usual part. When we talk about China or India we rarely talk about Chinese or Indians. We prefer to consider "diverse, high-value flows of business knowledge." I could not have made up this phrase if I had to, but that was not necessary: It is the work of one of our most popular commentators. The result of such preoccupations is that we know something about the yen or the yuan and Chinese car plants and the Tokyo capital markets and all else just listed, but not much about the Chinese or the Japanese. These are not three-dimensional people to us. Asians know this. It is part of what they assume about Westerners. In this respect, little has changed since the late nineteenth century. The Asia in our minds resembles a disassembled machine—nuts and bolts. It is long on data (the lowest form of knowledge) and short, very short, on understanding (the highest, the best we can ever do).

The notion that best illustrates the intellectual folly this kind of thinking produces is called Chindia. It is quintessentially utilitarian. It signifies at once the comparative treatment of China and India while telling us to think of more than two billion people as one immense mass of unindividuated humanity. It may produce all manner of useful information about cost-effectiveness, labor rates, property statutes, and other such matters, but there is no room in it for histories, religions, institutions, or an almost infinite variety of humanity in both countries, never mind the two together.

We have exhausted this way of thinking. We hold the far end of a thread that was spun a couple of centuries back. How much more do our modes of thinking obscure than they reveal, we must ask. We require a new way of understanding, one that gives us access to the whole as against its visible, material parts.

An acquaintance, the chief executive in Asia of a prominent American company, once took away from the Chindia discourse this thought: "India is 'over-democratized.' Hard to do business with them."

We were at dinner in an elegant grillroom.

"I thought the problem had more to do with 'under,' " I replied.

"Nope. What India needs is a Deng Xiaoping."

"Which Deng?" I asked. "Deng the practiced commissar, remorseless like most of the others? Or Deng the elf, the magician-reformist we invented in our newspapers?"

The conversation turned, of necessity, to other things. This did not matter. Over time my acquaintance made the point so often I began to see it was part of his standard presentation to visiting clients—wise, lateral thinking from a seasoned dweller in the unfathomable East. And that is what mattered. The man I describe had power within the corporate universe. He was listened to. And this is where our technocratic discourse on Asia leads us. It is the problem of the irrationality of the hyperrational. "Voltaire's bastards" is the term we use for those of such persuasions, and it does not seem too strong. It is with such exchanges in mind that I briefly note matters these pieces will and will not address.

ONE EVENING IN DELHI not long before I began writing these essays, the National Gallery of Modern Art opened a retrospective of the photographs of Raghu Rai. The households of the capital's elite must have been empty, for everyone who was anyone seemed to be there—cabinet ministers by the carload, literary figures, diplomats, artists, film and television people, journalists galore. It was tasteful glitter. Indians seem better at it than anyone. It seems something of the gift that comes of standing midway between East and West—a part of each, never wholly one or the other.

Rai deserved the occasion. He was born in 1942 and made his first photograph, "A Baby Donkey near Delhi," in 1965. He has gone on to shoot India as it lives and breathes for more than forty years. In his greatest black-and-white years, he caught it the way Cartier-Bresson caught China in the late 1940s: The pictures are with you even if you are unsure if you have seen them. Rai's India in dozens of grainy grays depicting the vast floodplains, the villages and cities, the shorelines and slums— Rai's India is everybody's in that his imagery is universal.

Conversing in the course of the evening, Rai told a story about going to Arles for an exhibition many years earlier and having to defend his decision to begin using a panoramic camera—a peculiar strategy at the time. It was the change in method that made him, for it was then he began producing the long, broad prints that give us the dust, struggle, commotion, vitality, and variety of India as it is.

"India is a horizontal experience for me," Rai said. "There

are so many layers that exist side by side and must be captured all at once."

Rai did not seem to think he had said anything extraordinary, but I did. I mention this encounter because Rai's method is my own. If I were a photographer, I, too, would use a panoramic lens, setting the f-stop at, say, 32: The glass gives you great breadth, and the small aperture sharp resolution and depth of field.

I left New York for Asia in 1981. Most correspondents might serve a tour in, say, Beijing and then perhaps another in Tokyo or Bangkok or Delhi, and then they would return to head office or move on to Paris or Buenos Aires. I drew a different straw. This book arises, then, from more than a quarter century of living and working among Asians and studying and reading about them (and reading some of the things they have written). A lot of conversing, reporting, and writing has accumulated by a slow accretion. The questions were countless in the beginning, and then, one by one, they either got answered or got dropped from the docket as being of lesser consequence. Over time a certain focus emerged. In the end, or at least for now, the questions have come to three, as the shape of this book suggests.

THE FIRST OF THESE essays might just as well have been called "What Does It Mean to Be Modern?" because this is the question posed. I chose "Calligraphy and Clocks" to underscore the most basic distinction that must be grasped if one is to understand Asia in the modern era. "Spirit" and "things" are two terms from the Japanese, but variants appear elsewhere— and emphatically the distinction does, whether or not it is named. There is tradition, culture, belief, practice, what we would today term "values"; and there are railroads, steel mills, shoehorns, cars, kitchen gadgets, computers—extension cords, indeed. There is nothing especially Asian about drawing a line between the two and treating things, the objects and technologies of modern life, as if they materialized from nowhere. This, indeed, is what they did in Asia. But Asia's attempt at such a separation in the mid-nineteenth century, beginning in Japan and China, is the very core of its experience of "the modern." I consider it the single most fateful mistake modern Asia has ever made. It produced a crisis—of belief, meaning, and identity—that has endured for 150 years. Only now does this crisis ebb—the mark of our moment.

In the course of some years I noticed the peculiar relations Asians have with their own histories. This is the subject of the second essay, "The Buddhas at Qixia." There was, so often, a dysfunction. Over more years I came to relate this to the modern experience, the encounter with the West. There was apparent causality. China offers the most graphic illustration. Its record on this score in the twentieth century is one of sheer wreckage: Believe this but not that, read this, no longer that; no, read and believe all of that and forget all of this; no again, read and believe something altogether otherwise. All this was in response to how China should be modern. One does not marvel that psychotherapy is now catching on quickly among the Chinese, with psychological counselors (though not psychiatrists) taking training via the Internet. One marvels that they got by so long without such a palliative.

An extreme case, China, but beyond the matter of degree not unusual. Why this? What did the great encounter with the industrial West do to jar loose so many people from their pasts? This is the second question.

To introduce the third essay, "The Skyward Garden," I will return briefly to that evening in Delhi I spent with Raghu Rai.

"Photography has been a Western medium," Rai had said. "We've all been influenced by Western photographers for a long time. But there comes a saturation point for any artist in any medium. Mine came when I began using the panoramic camera. I did that for a specific reason."

What was that reason? In the particular, it was to get India down in gelatin prints the truest way he could. More generally, the "saturation point" was the moment Rai stopped listening to the West, stopped importing anyone's method, stopped being anyone's student or protégé, and began to respond to the world as he saw it in front of him. India had begun to tell him how and what to think about India.

The thought at the core of this final essay, the possibility of a post-Western world, derives from a piece I wrote for *The Washington Quarterly*, one based on time spent in Iran and published in the spring of 2000. The question I pose now is simple and complicated all at once. Can Asia understand itself without reference to the West? To put it another way, are Asians evolving an idea of progress that does not arise solely from ours—an idea that might be of use to all of us?

All knowledge involves an act of comparing, it has been said; to incorporate and transform what is "other" is how the universe works—its most basic mechanism. But that brief exchange with Raghu Rai suggests that Asia is discovering that the habits of more than a century are no longer enough. The impulse to know themselves anew is palpably abroad among Asians. My encounter with Rai is but the tiniest example, resembling the instant his shutter exposes a frame.

I HAVE ALREADY IMPLIED the three countries on which I propose to concentrate. Japan, China, India: Do I mean cultures? Civilizations? Societies? Nations? Something of all is the best answer. These essays concern thinking, feeling, ways of seeing, pasts. The countries I have named seemed to offer the best ways to peer into these matters. I do not intend to limit the frame of reference, however. My choices are meant to illuminate beyond their borders.

My list may come across as odd. Japan and India between the same covers? As I refined my questions down to what I considered an irreducible three, I put the countries where I would primarily apply them to a few friends.

"The cultures that have produced epics," one replied.

I had not thought of this and considered it not much more than a curiosity. Then I began to wonder. The thought perhaps suggests a coherence and continuity in these three that is useful in bringing us to a more fundamental understanding of what we call the East. A shared path, let us say, plainly marked. Certainly it was interesting, as the work and years went along, to discover that Indians are having some of the same conversations about themselves in the early twenty-first century that the Japanese had in the second half of the nineteenth.

WHAT DO WE MEAN BY "the West" and "the East"? Herodotus wrote about these entities two and a half millennia ago. He was concerned with Greeks and Persians, among others. For many centuries thereafter the West claimed Greece as the fountainhead of its heritage, although we have now come to recognize that there was nothing especially Western, as opposed to Eastern, about Hellenic civilization. Later the West came to signify the Christian world—a religious concept. In the nineteenth century the West took shape as a political construct, and this was truly a matter of knowing oneself by way of the "other": There was the West, and there were the Russians in "the East." In the twentieth century, of course, the political notion turned military. At present it is political and military. The Christianity of the piece looks shaky, even if some Americans cling to it, and the whole apparatus is making its way eastward from "the Atlantic world" into the old Russian sphere of influence.

Fungible, as notions go, we have to say. So is "the East." "The Moors," as we were taught to call them long ago, made it all the way to central France, of course, and the Ottoman Empire reached Hungary. By the eighteenth century, eastern Europe was emphatically "East" (and so not a very desirable place to be) to western Europeans. In 1946, Churchill famously drew his curtain across it from the Baltic to the Adriatic. The East was "red," just as the Chinese soon told us. Even in places it was not—Japan, most of Southeast Asia—we worried it would turn the dreaded hue, and the East became a contentious and eventually bloody Cold War theater.

For the purposes of these essays, we can try to keep matters simple. By "the East" we mean those regions conventionally known as West Asia, South Asia, and East Asia. As to "the West," my reference is to the nineteenth-century industrial West as it arrived and extended its influence in Asia. This was the colonizing West in the case of India, and in China and Japan it was the influence-exerting West of the Opium Wars and Commodore Perry respectively.

Instantly there are complications. One of Portugal's great nineteenth-century novelists, José Maria de Eça de Queirós, complained this way about the arrival of northern Europe in the less-developed south: "Here we import everything," he wrote in *The Maias*, his best-known work. "Ideas, laws, philosophies, theories, plots, aesthetics, sciences, style, industries, fashions, manners, jokes, everything arrives in crates by steamship." So the colonizer of da Gama's day was among the colonized once the industrial world started stretching out. We will have to bear this kind of irony in mind.

A Japanese scholar named Naoki Sakai has an interesting solution to such conundrums. Forget about borders, geographies, and all the rest, he argues. An Asian is anyone in whom we find "some effect of social adversity or a trait of alienation from the alleged ideal image of a Westerner . . . regardless of his or her physiognomy, linguistic heritage, claimed ethnicity, or habitual characteristics." To be "other" or oppressed is to be

Asian, then. If we are not part of the industrial West, we are "Asian." It is to stretch the word beyond its elasticity. The Portuguese of Eça de Queirós were Asian by this definition. On the other hand, one can follow Sakai's reasoning. Europeans are said to have invented the term "Asia"—by way of *asu*, the ancient Akkadian for "sunrise"—to distinguish themselves from the great "other" of the East, meaning everyone else.

Beyond this introduction, I will not burden readers or clutter these pages with quotation marks around any but the most needful references to East and West. They would be justified, however, for these terms are confining, uncomfortable, and given to causing misunderstandings. Equally, they are losing what usefulness they may have had for an interim of human history. After all his travels and all the questions he posed, Herodotus concluded that the business of East and West was "imaginary." The line he referred to was drawn by humans. For a long time now we have simply lost track of this. We have erred in thinking the divide is eternal—ever there, ever to be there, somehow (and somewhere) etched into the earth. Now we enter a time when we can see from another perspective and see the truth of things and of ourselves.

AN ALTERED PERSPECTIVE will prove essential if we are to succeed in what I choose to call a post-Western era. It will reveal many things to us. We will better understand the East and ourselves, its place in a new epoch and our own. We will recognize the wisdom of Herodotus in describing history as a matter of alternating movements, and we will see that we are witnessing one. If we are determined, we will see the West from the East, and such distance will be especially revelatory. Just as the nineteenth century required Asians to invent a certain self, we will come face-to-face with the constructed nature of our Western selves. And we will see how a new era will require us to change these selves—meaning no less than ourselves.

An Asian alive in the nineteenth century would have concluded that he or she lived in someone else's century. It belonged to the West because all that was modern did. "We are all modern now," as a Chinese friend once put it, and this alters more or less everything. We do not stand at the start of "an Asian century" to match the one just passed, commonly considered "American." Role reversal is not at issue. We mean reversals of another kind. We will find that what were once Asia's disadvantages are now often its advantages. By the same measure, what were once the West's great strengths are now its challenges; what propelled us at one moment in history may restrain us in this, another. This portends neither an "Asian" nor any kind of "Eastern century." To think in such terms implies an idea of power that is passé. The best we can say is that our time is post-Western. It is our turn in the West to say the new century is simply someone else's, other than altogether our own.

I HAVE CALLED THESE pieces essays because the term best describes their intent. They are in an order I think useful, and ideas introduced in one occasionally carry over into another, but they are not chapters, with a sequence. They do not offer comprehensive "coverage" of any topic—there is no such ambition. To return to the original sense of the term (Montaigne's), these are attempts, forays, explorations. There is more, always, to be said.

To suggest some fundamental aspects of "Asia as it is," the Asia before our eyes, is admittedly a modest endeavor. I have tried to accomplish the task by way of three questions and an exploration of the many answers engendered as I posed them here and there and now and then over many years. These essays are the result. They are written with an ambition best expressed by Amartya Sen, the Indian Nobelist, when dedicating one of his recent books. He wrote, he said, "with the hope of a world less imprisoned by illusion."

Readings

Coker, Christopher. *Twilight of the West*. Boulder, CO, 1998.
Harootunian, Harry. *History's Disquiet*. New York, 2000.
———. *Overcome by Modernity*. Princeton, NJ, 2000.
Sakai Naoki. "You Asians." In *"We Asians": Between Past and Future*. Singapore, 2000.
Scheler, Max. *Ressentiment*. Milwaukee, 2007.
Schorske, Carl E. *Thinking With History*. Princeton, NJ, 1998.

Calligraphy and Clocks

What they wanted was only what they could see.
—JIWEI CI, *Dialectic of the Chinese Revolution* (1994)

1

KITAKYUSHU TRANSLATES AS "North Kyushu," and that is where the city lies: atop Japan's large southern island, where a narrow sea separates Kyushu from Honshu, the long main island where most Japanese live.

Kitakyushu has an interesting past. Until the turn of the twentieth century it was a collection of five villages. Then everything changed. The villages were near coalfields and had the makings of a port; Kyushu had no earthquakes. In 1901, when Japan was hard at work making itself modern, the Meiji government chose a village called Yahata and built Japan's first steel mill in it. Many companies followed: coke ovens, petroleum refineries, chemical producers. We can reckon the prewar progress of the villages easily: On August 9, 1945, they were to receive the Truman administration's second atom bomb. Cloudy skies forced American pilots to resort to Plan B: Plan B being Nagasaki.

In the decades after the war, reconstruction and economic growth became an idée fixe in Japan. This is well enough known. "Catching up with the West," it was called; the Japanese nicknamed it "GNPism." Kitakyushu, fair to say, became somewhat irrational during this period. Thousands of new companies set up shop along Dokai Bay and made cars and everything else that required steel. By this time the Yahata works were part of Nippon Steel, Japan's most celebrated corporation during its "miracle" years. And the image of the blast furnace glowing against the darkness half a century earlier fascinated the Japanese. It was totemic. A history text published in 1961 described the mill's earliest days this way:

> Machines working with a growling sound, blast furnaces smelting and brightening a night sky, and everything is vivid and vital. Yahata is called the capital of steel.

Kitakyushu became Japan's fourth-largest industrial center after the war, and in time the five villages were incorporated into the city we know today. Pictures from the postwar period are highly evocative. They show the flat roofs of old wooden houses, huddled low and hard by one another so that they look a bit Cubist, and, all around them, looming smokestacks looking like bunches of grotesque dandelions. A retired Nippon Steel executive I knew once estimated that there had been more than a thousand industrial chimneys in the city. They produced what became known locally as *nama ito no kemuri*, "the smoke of seven colors," each color identified with one of the big industries. In the old pictures the smoke covered the city like a quilt of mismatched hues, so that the squat rooftops were only here and there visible, and parts of the smokestacks were not visible at all.

The old executive, whose name was Kenichi Fujimoto, recalled some of this one afternoon in a community center where retirees gathered. He had worked for Nippon Steel's chemical subsidiary. "We were proud of our seven colors," this kindly man remembered, "and that the smoke in the air was also in our lungs."

"The Japanese miracle" is the name we give to the country's not-quite-rational postwar behavior. There was nothing miraculous, of course, about it. The "miracle" was the consequence of a compulsion. Nothing seemed to dent Kitakyushu's pride and drive. Ships' propellers dissolved if they were too long at anchor in Dokai Bay. Housewives hung laundry out in the morning, and when they collected it at day's end there might be holes in it. Dust fall—a mix of soot and chemicals—collected like snow on the windowsills of local schools. These pollutants peaked in the 1960s. Illnesses—respiratory problems, skin and intestinal diseases, cancers—did not reach their high for another decade. "By 1990," Fujimoto said, "we had 100,000 people on compensation."

Kitakyushu has had a happy ending, as these things go. It remains an industrial city, but now it is clean and exceptionally "green." You sense, as you make your way around the city and its gardens and the forested hills that used to separate the old villages, that people are as proud of the air and water now as they once were to see both befouled. Some fundamental change in thinking has occurred.

But there, in what was once the village of Yahata, the old steel plant still stands. It is the strangest of monuments now: The original works were rebuilt after the war, and then later the mill was decommissioned and (mostly) torn down. What stands now—a smokestack, three tall boilers, the blast furnace, and the Erector-set tower around it—is a replica of a rebuild. All that remains of the original mill is the brick-lined core, the cold heart of the thing where the orange glow that so captivated Japan once sent sparks and light outward. It is enough, it seems. Atop the tower an old sign still announces in block numerals to the rest of the city: "1901." The curator of a museum next door explained that the government was developing a new idea around Japan—"industrial tourism," he called it. Yahata was to be a main stop on the route.

While I was talking to Fujimoto, the retired chemical executive, a few of his friends joined us. They seemed, this roomful of men in their seventies, dedicated salarymen to a one. But they were a divided lot. They stood by their accomplishments after the war, but each was divided within himself. The hint of remorse—of sheepishness for having followed a path blindly—was as palpable as the pride.

I mentioned an old photograph I had seen—a well-known

image in Kitakyushu. It showed the Yahata works on its opening day. In the foreground, as if in a class picture, were a few
dozen dignitaries in formal attire. The image was famous
mostly because one of those in it was Ito Hirobumi, Japan's first
prime minister. Ito had come from Tokyo for the occasion.

All the old Nippon Steel men knew the picture. I wondered
aloud what it meant to them. A man named Nobuyoshi Tanaka
replied: "This was the country's first steel plant—an integrated
steel plant. We were poor fishermen and farmers, you see. This
is where we began to make ourselves modern."

ASIA IS ONE," a Japanese thinker named Kakuzo Okakura
declared long ago in a book called *The Ideals of the East.*
Okakura was a curious figure: urbane and traveled, addicted to
Egyptian cigarettes, a friend, adviser, and co-collector among
the nineteenth-century Bostonians who first brought Asian art
to America. Like many other gentlemen of the time, Okakura
would dress in a Western suit or in kimono, depending on the
occasion. He was an early example of a certain type: an Asian
who is also an Orientalist in the way he sees things, an Asian
who knows how Asia looks to Westerners and comes to accommodate that way of seeing—in whole or in part, publicly or pri-
vately, genuinely or because it suits his purpose.

Okakura made his observation in 1904, three years after
Yahata lit its fires. It has enjoyed little fashion since. The
Greater East Asia Co-Prosperity Sphere did the idea no good.
In our time, to see Asia as one is considered something un-
comprehending Westerners do. Religions, cultures, languages,
philosophic traditions; islands, plains, mountains, and valleys;
jungle, desert, snowcapped peaks; cultivated court folk and
primitive tribes: Wherein could we find Asia to be one?

Neither has much credence been accorded Okakura's corollary thought: Japan must be credited for gathering all the strands of Asia and weaving them into a cord. "It is in Japan alone," Okakura wrote, "that the historic wealth of Asiatic culture can be consecutively studied through its treasured specimens." And then: "The history of Japanese art becomes thus the history of Asiatic ideals—the beach where each successive wave of Eastern thought has left its sand-ripple as it beat against the national consciousness."

Japan had absorbed influences from many places over many centuries by the time Okakura wrote. It was in its way a gathering spot, although everything that came was then changed. Equally, 1904 was a special time for the Japanese: They were about to defeat the Russian navy in the East China Sea and claim a place among world powers, the first Asians to do so. We may discount Okakura's thesis, but as with any idea we should be aware of the moment to which it gave expression.

Today we must hold Okakura's thought up to the light once again. And Asia is indeed one, we find—or, without making too fine a point of it, we can say there are at least features of oneness in it. Okakura had it wrong in many ways; certainly he would not mean "Asia is one" the way someone would consider the idea today. Let "Asia" denote part of the planet in its complexity and diversity. But to be Asian also means to be Eastern, and this means something unifying: It means to be other than Western. For a long time it has meant to be excluded, or— much better—to think of oneself as excluded. Okakura concluded that Asia was one in its weakness.

In most of Asia, weakness led to an acceptance without questioning of all things Western. High among these was the West's recently formed idea of progress. Asia's task was to fall in line with this idea—to run so as to catch up. But again a paradox: As Okakura saw it, Asia's challenge was soon one of restoration— the regaining of a lost validity—and in this he was prophetic by a century. "Life lies ever in the return to self," he wrote.

———

THE NOTION OF PROGRESS today is highly suspect. Today we truly must wonder as to the validity of that great ark of assumptions afloat upon a single term. This does not matter just now. The point to be made has to do with when in history Asia had its first substantial contact with the modern. This was in the middle of the nineteenth century, when the idea of progress, all things proceeding in a logical and legible line, was hitting its highest note. The modern, by and large, came suddenly to Asia; there was an all-at-onceness to it. And all that was modern, all that progressed, the very concept that framed these things, belonged to someone else. Westerners often miss this aspect of Asian thinking. Bessemer, Daguerre, Henry Ford: They were all part of "our" tradition, Westerners would say— "their" tradition, as Asians would put it. We are advancing beyond so simple a formulation, but for a long time it has produced different relationships between people and modern things. For a long time it was not the same for a Westerner or an Easterner to drive a car or wear leather shoes. For a Westerner these things came from his or her past; for an Asian they were from somebody else's. This sensation, this experience of ordinary life, echoes down to us in the present, however faintly. It is another thing that has made Asia one.

There is no other way to explain what I have suggested was the madness of Kitakyushu in its postwar phase. The term is fair (and not ill intended). What happened in Kitakyushu and numerous other Japanese cities is not much different from what happened, say, in nineteenth-century England and America. They had their not-altogether-rational messes and degradations, too. But again, the "when" of something cannot be left out. One reason Kitakyushu went slightly mad was that it was doing in the 1950s what "they" had done a hundred years earlier. It accounts for a drive that led people to act irrationally in favor of needs that arose elsewhere: emotional needs, psychological needs. A sublimation took place. There is nothing Asian about any of this: The same would have occurred in reverse. We associate it with Asia simply because it took place later in history and we could watch it with greater awareness.

We come again to Okakura. However much Japan may once have been the collector of other Asian cultures, in the modern era it became something else. The first non-Western nation to modernize, by the turn of the twentieth century it was the model for others to emulate. Okakura was antiquarian in this regard. By his time Japan was important among Asians not for what it had absorbed from them but for what it had absorbed from the West and what it could give them: a way to manage the experience of the modern.

IN BEIJING, I sometimes used to go on autumn afternoons to a teahouse on Nanchang Jie, a tree-lined street a short walk from Tian'anmen Square. It was an old place made of brick—late Qing, the tea man thought—with a low facade and a plain wooden door that revealed nothing of the courtyard within and all the rooms giving onto it. Wang Zhenjiang was a retired aeronautical engineer in his sixties, and he kept his teahouse as a gathering place for friends and the friends of friends (such as I was). We used to call it "Uncle Wang's," and I went there to meet scholars, writers, Buddhist revivalists, tea connoisseurs, neighborhood familiars.

Uncle Wang was being evicted. It was a common story across China at this time. In the capital, most of the *hutong*, the narrow lanes lined with courtyard houses, had already been bulldozed. In the south of the city I once watched an entire community, block upon block of it, turned out in a couple of days to make way for the plaza of a new railway station. To be evicted in this way is to be *chai*ed. It is part of China's way of modernizing.

Just before the Beijing Olympics in the summer of 2008,

the municipal authorities did something curious. There were neighborhoods slated for demolition that they had not had time to *chai*. So they sent work crews to erect brick walls that obscured the old urban hamlets from view. They were there, part of what made Beijing Beijing, but no one coming for the games was to see them. This is China: a vast field of aspiration—aspiration well mixed with conflict. It wants to be seen and known not as it is but as it wishes itself to be.

The fate of Uncle Wang's teahouse was the consequence of a certain love and hate the Chinese had come to feel toward themselves as they had once been, as they were, and as they wanted to be. The more *hutong* and old houses the authorities tore down, the more treasured were those remaining. I had a friend who lived in a rebuilt replica of a *hutong* house that had been *chai*ed: The original came down, then a change of heart, and another one like it went up. The nostalgia, then, was merely keeping pace with the modernization—or became, indeed, a feature of the process. This was so even among the authorities doing the tearing down. Behind Wang's eviction was a Communist Party official who wanted to build a traditional house where the teahouse stood. There would be modern comforts, but the old brick facade would remain, as would the distance between inside and outside—a few feet when measured with tape, vast in the abstract, as a psychological distinction. The trees would remain, too—the rows of French plane trees the Chinese planted in many cities many years ago.

"I'm among the neighborhood's last survivors," Wang said once as we walked through the house. He paused, gazing out at the old tile roof and a drain fashioned from plastic pipe hanging from it. Then he said: "If you haven't got a past, you haven't got a future, either—you can't go forward."

The thought turned Wang to his childhood in Dalian, the city in the northeast once known as Port Arthur. He still traveled down sometimes on the overnight train to see family and friends. It was not the same, Wang said. Dalian had long served the gritty industrial cities to its north. There had been layers of the past—the past of the Russians, then the past of the Japanese once they defeated the Russians in 1905. Dalian's architecture had had this history embedded into it. Now there were only bits of that and bits of the Communist past—the ever-soiled six-story apartment buildings one finds in Chinese cities, although these were going, too.

"It was our mayor in the 1990s, Bo Xilai," Wang mentioned.

Bo, indeed, was famous around China. His father, Bo Yibo, had been an early revolutionary fighter, later served as a minister, was purged during the Cultural Revolution, and was finally rehabilitated under Deng Xiaoping. Bo the younger made a name for himself by taking office in 1992 and leveling as much of Dalian as he could. He had a slogan that made him something of a *personage* among the mainland's mayors, a man to study and emulate. *Chai chai kan*, it went. "Tear it down and see what happens."

Wang laughed when the slogan came up. "There's a pun in it," he explained. "In Mandarin it sounds like 'Guess what's next.'"

As urban-renewal strategies go, it is novel—we have to give Bo Xilai this much. But we must also pose the question raised: From what springs the impulse to demolish most of a metropolis without having much of a plan as to how to replace it? As in Kitakyushu, there is more to Dalian's story as a star of Chinese modernization than economic need.

Walking in the city once, I strayed from the broad avenues Bo had built (without much thought of pedestrians) and wandered into one of the quarters remaining from old Dalian. I ended up on a potholed lane talking to a fishmonger in an outdoor market. Around us were rows of old workers' housing, probably from the Japanese era, shabby but solidly built. Bo Xilai was no longer mayor, but I doubted the neighborhood had much more time.

The fishmonger's name was Zhang Dengya. He wore a

bagged-out tweed jacket and was happy enough to talk. It started to rain, and as we conversed I helped Zhang with an intricate mess of filthy beach umbrellas he was tying into place with string and wire above his fish tanks.

"All this change in Dalian," I said. "What do people think of it?"

"We have to change," Zhang replied without looking up from his tanks. "At first it upsets you, but you get used to it. For me, I'll take it at . . . at a thousand miles a day—faster, even."

"It's so necessary as that, Mr. Zhang?"

"If we don't change, foreigners will look down on us."

"You really think that?"

"Appearance is everything," Zhang said flatly.

We stopped talking for a moment.

Then Zhang asked, "What do Americans think of Chinese?"

"Most of us know China's growing quickly," I replied, "but I'm not sure we know a lot more. How Chinese people think and feel, for instance."

"How we think and feel? That's easy. Make China prosperous, make China powerful."

TO BE RICH AND STRONG is not a new idea, of course. The Japanese elevated *fukoku kyohei*, "rich nation, strong army," to a national slogan as they set about making themselves modern. Rich and strong eventually led to Kitakyushu, just as the thought led to the fishmonger's view of things in Dalian. And as the fishmonger made plain, to desire wealth and strength is not something one can do all on one's own: You have to encounter someone richer and stronger to do that.

The Japanese were not short of slogans. In the 1870s one of the best-known Japanese of his time, Fukuzawa Yukichi, made famous the idea of *bunmei kaika*, "civilization and enlightenment." This was different from the prevailing preoccupation with rich and strong. It meant emulating the best of the West.

Bunmei, civilization, was a term Fukuzawa coined himself. He defined it as "that which advances man's knowledge and virtue," and the modern West had a lot to teach Japan in these regards, he considered. Fukuzawa was much celebrated during his time—and remains so today—but civilization and enlightenment eventually got him into trouble. His critics accused him of advocating the sale of Japan's soul. Then he went in a strange direction himself: To be civilized and enlightened also meant following Westerners as they built empires, and this led to a Japanese version of *la mission civilisatrice.* By the time he died, the year the Yahata Steel Works opened, Fukuzawa (a Kyushu man, coincidentally) had turned again: Awash in material things, he came to think, Japan was in need of moral and spiritual renewal.

To me it has long seemed that the most important phrase to emerge from Japan's early experience of the modern is one not much talked about. It is *wakon yosai,* meaning "Japanese spirit, Western technology" or "knowledge"—or, as I prefer for its simplicity, "Western things." I do not know why this slogan, which seems to date from early in the Meiji era, is no longer much recalled. This may be because the distinction was so ingrained for so long among the Japanese as to be automatic. It may also be that the notion of the Japanese spirit was so profoundly discredited in 1945 that no one other than an extreme rightist wants to go anywhere near such a thought. But I have also suspected that the spirit-and-things formulation enjoys a modest reputation precisely because it has had such an extraordinary effect—not just in Japan and not just long ago, but across much of Asia and now. So we should consider this idea carefully. The distinction it makes has helped to give us, among other things, World War II, Kitakyushu and all that it exemplified after the war, Dalian and all that the Chinese are doing to destroy their own habitat. Even further afield, we find the same thought embedded in Iran's desire to develop nuclear technology. It is all of a piece: variations on a theme that has sounded in Asia for a century and a half.

The original term was different and the same all at once. Japan, the great borrower, did most of its borrowing from the Middle Kingdom for the millennium and a half before Meiji, and so the idea first arose as *wakon kansai*—Japanese spirit, Chinese things. No one knows when this was. By tradition the idea is attributed to a ninth-century scholar, but it may have been set down as late as the eighteenth or early nineteenth century, not long before Japan was to rotate its gaze, begin the great borrowing that made it modern, and change the phrase to match the times.

CONTEMPORARY ACCOUNTS OF Commodore Matthew Perry's arrival in a bay south of Tokyo give us some curious detail. The shogunate had an idea he was coming and knew well enough his intent to "open" Japan. But the local fishermen who first spotted Perry's "black ships" one morning during the hazy summer of 1853 knew nothing of these affairs. The Americans spotted several fishing boats from the town of Shimoda just as they were hurrying back to the harbor. Among the town folk there was something like mayhem. They had never seen steamships and did not know what to make of the smoke on the horizon. From a hilltop they concluded some of their own boats had caught fire, or the sea itself was afire, or volcanoes had arisen from the ocean.

It is a telling vignette. By all accounts there was a measure of what we would today call shock and awe. Natsume Soseki, the great writer of Meiji Japan and a great writer in any time or place, put it well in his diary many years later. "People say that Japan was awakened thirty years ago," he wrote, "but it was awakened by a fire bell and jumped out of bed. It was not a genuine awakening but a totally confused one."

Perry did not stun and confuse the Japanese and later get

his treaties signed by brandishing Bacon, Descartes, Kant, or Jefferson—not directly, anyway. What he had to show them came from Robert Fulton, Samuel Morse, and Samuel Colt. They were things—steam engines, telegraphs, and guns—and the immense power that derived from possessing these inventions. Years later, after Japan had mastered much, Fukuzawa went straight to the point in professing the source of his pride. "As I consider all the other peoples of the Orient," he wrote, "there is no other nation which has the ability or the courage to navigate a steamship across the Pacific after a period of five years of experience in navigation and engineering."

Even as "Chinese things" was switched to "Western things," Japan had a little time to consider the reformulation. In 1824, a quarter of a century before Perry arrived, the shogunate detained a British sailor washed ashore from a whaling ship. It was taken as a portent: The Westerners were surely coming. The following year a scholar named Aizawa Seishisai published a book called *Shinron*—The New Theses, or New Proposals. "Today the alien barbarians of the West, the lowly organs of the legs and feet of the world, are dashing about across the seas, trampling other countries underfoot," the treatise began, "and daring, with their squinting eyes and limping feet, to override the noble nations." Fukuzawa put the point more delicately some decades later. "When I examine which excels the other as to wealth, armament, and general well-being," he wrote, "I have to put the Orient below the Occident." It came down to "number and reason," Fukuzawa thought: In these were Asians deficient.

Between the xenophobe and the cultivated gentleman, we need to note, the difference was primarily one of style. Both men took the separation of spirit and things as a given, a starting point in anyone's understanding of Japan's predicament as Westerners arrived to make the sand ripple anew. Rather crucially, both the early anti-Westerner and the later, worldlier thinker also held spirit to be the higher value, the point of privilege, the more precious of the two apprehensions.

In this latter way one almost prefers the crudity of Aizawa, the late shogunate's philosopher, to the gentler Fukuzawa. The older man got straight to the point: There was nothing noble about the West when viewed from Japanese shores. The West was method and no more. And how vastly inferior to spirit was this. Fukuzawa had far more occasion to think this through. Two and a half centuries of *sakoku*, the official policy of isolation, had ended by his time. But Fukuzawa came to a precisely congruent conclusion nonetheless. Aizawa's legs and feet became Fukuzawa's number and reason. It amounted to the same thing, the thing that shocked (and soon enough captivated) the Shimoda fishing folk: the sheer mechanics of material superiority.

We may speculate as to whether there might have been another way to conceive of the dilemma. Emphatically there was, but we can leave this thought for now, the what-if of it. This was a defining moment, as we would say today. The tense strings that suspend all of Asia's modern experience are wound on the pegs of "spirit and things." Once this was fixed as the frame of modern thinking, there was only one way forward. The spirit was precious and to be defended, while modern things were to be made cold use of. Ends and means were two, unjoined. The Japanese are well-known for the strategy, even in our time: Let the foreigner in so as to keep him out. In a not-altogether-different context, there is the way Lampedusa put it in *The Leopard*, the great novel of the colliding old and new set in nineteenth-century Sicily. "If we want things to stay as they are," the noted line goes, "things will have to change." Consider Italy as another "late developer" among nations, and it is not so strange that the thought appeared in two such apparently different places.

We can count many events and much history among the

consequences of this consciousness of spirit and things. World War II is among the more obvious examples. One wants to diminish neither politics nor power nor history nor human agency in understanding it. But the Japanese fought it, as is well enough known, in the name of spirit. In this sense the war was the culmination of Japan's collision with the modern—the proving event in which a pure spirit was to triumph over mere things. The thought runs through many of the old diaries and the poetry of the kamikaze pilots. This is why, beyond all the deaths and destruction, the outcome instantly weighed so heavily on the Japanese. A structure of consciousness collapsed. Spirit was suddenly nothing; things had proven out. It led, plainly enough, straight to Kitakyushu: Things were all that remained to the postwar Japanese. So began our familiar associations with Japan during the so-called miracle decades: a people methodically given only to making things of all imaginable variety.

Something else happened that applies to others besides the Japanese. What follows when people attempt to separate their identity and culture from an incoming way of life, as if imported things were merely objects, with no tradition implicit in them? We can carry the answer far around Asia. Identity and culture come quickly to stand with a velvet rope around them: They are museum pieces. Or—choose your simile—they are pickled, like some kind of squid specimen or a human organ immersed in a jar of formaldehyde. They are no longer living. Early in the Meiji era the government invented a word, *dento*, to designate officially recognized tradition—the approved wellspring of modernizing Japan's culture and identity. The country would be topsy-turvy with the arriving new in the decades to come. And there at the center would serenely sit *dento*—tea drinking, flower arranging, inking calligraphy on rice paper, throwing pots by an ancient method.

The self-consciousness tells us much. One cannot stand

above one's identity, godlike, and preserve it, create it, or even cultivate it. If you attempt any of these, you are larger than it is, and this cannot logically be. In such instances, your identity is not what you are concocting. You are in reality the person doing the concocting. Therein is who you are and what you have made of yourself. And for you the modern has truly begun. You are someone new; you have walked out on the thin ice of existence as an act of incessant becoming. The only alternative is nostalgia—the "once was" as against the "as it is."

CHINA HAD ALREADY HEARD the fire bell of arriving Westerners by the time Perry steamed into Shimoda in 1853. The Qing dynasty had lost the Opium Wars to the British a dozen years earlier. This was to change China as much as—probably more than, if such a comparison is possible—the chain of events touched off by Perry's black ships. The treaties imposed on the emperor Daoguang in 1842 marked the point of departure for the Middle Kingdom, as China had long thought of itself: From that moment on, the term itself acquired a coloring of history or nostalgia or irony. China was not to be the middle of anything anymore, but to join all the others dwelling on somebody else's periphery.

The Opium Wars remain a point of reference among the Chinese today, recalled more palpably than anything Americans or Europeans would typically know of their 1840s. They were the starting point for the convulsion that is modern Chinese history. It was the moment the Chinese had to pose a question already suggested: If this is not Zhongguo, the Central Realm, then what does it mean to be Chinese? The Japanese, by comparison, faced no such conundrum—not then: At the time of Perry's arrival, one dwelled in this or that *han*, this or that feudal domain. The Chinese and the Middle Kingdom had far to fall in this respect.

It is curious, too, to reflect that the same material things that stunned the Japanese did a yet more thorough job in China: They were "thundering tubes," as the Japanese called guns, and steam engines in the bowels of paddle wheelers. China had been dealing with foreigners for centuries by the 1840s, but the earlier sort were Jesuits and diplomats. Now they came to deliver military defeat and the shock of suddenly realized inferiority. We can imagine this sensation easily enough today. It lies just below the surface of Chinese life and erupts through it routinely. The fishmonger in Dalian: He articulated neither more nor less than the echoes of the Opium Wars.

Interesting detail comes to us through the histories. As the British prosecuted their war for drugs—which is what the Opium Wars amounted to—they found along the coast a nascent industry: Chinese shipbuilders were far along in producing copies of Western vessels and naval artillery. Considering that the war had effectively run, full scale, only from the summer of 1840, this must be counted something of a feat. It implies a predisposition, a readiness to face the new, that is at odds with China's long habit of living by precedent. The past determined the future, under the Qing as under earlier dynasties. But the backdrop to the Opium Wars, the moment of China's frontal encounter with the modern, suggests the thought of something new had some validity.

Foreigners with hardware and money instead of New Testaments and diplomatic *portefeuilles* were not China's only, or even most pressing, problem in the mid-nineteenth century. To say the British applied the fatal blows to imperial rule is a lot like saying Americans toppled the Soviet Union. In both cases outside influence had something, maybe even much, to do with bringing the end nearer. In neither case would it be right to say foreigners were the primary doers of the deed. This kind of change always comes from within, however much others may wish to aggrandize themselves.

Scholars, intellectuals, bureaucrats, court mandarins—many

Chinese minds had been taken up with the Qing's increasingly evident failures since the late eighteenth century. These produced a sense of uncertainty, and then instability, even as life seemed to go on as it always had. The achievements of the Ming, the preceding dynasty, marked a high point in Chinese history. But these were at the core aesthetic and cultural accomplishments, even as they put China ahead of Europe in many respects. Less attentive were the Ming to practical matters, which is why they gave way to the Qing—Manchu from the north, tribal warriors for whom the practicalities of power counted more than artistic refinement. The Qing replaced the Ming in 1644. By the time British warships arrived two centuries later, it had already become apparent that China was not rising to some new task. The old examination system was not up to it. Administrative practice—read the old records to learn what to do—looked turgid and outdated. There was an alarming divide between city and village and much local corruption; quixotic cults threatened the throne's control. (Has the bell of familiarity rung yet?)

All this brought China to the brink of a momentous fracture. Until this time, and even during it, tradition was the wellspring of all authority and validity. A new idea was a reinterpretation of an old idea; a newly executed painting displayed (or failed to display) mastery of the style to which it alluded. All was lineage. But the lineage was not delivering. The Qing adopted China's way of doing things, but China's way appeared to lack a needed practicality. All ideas and solutions were still Chinese ideas and solutions, but was China properly equipped? Did China have it within itself to meet new challenges? No one could ask these questions: China's intellectual universe remained closed. But the moment to pose them seemed near, with or without the foreign factor, although we cannot go back and paint the British out of the picture.

The Opium Wars, then, are best seen as a catalyst. They

were, indeed, not unlike a jolt of electromagnetic energy run through a suspended solution. In an instant the Chinese conversation clarified.

THE CONVERSATION WAS transformed for the simple reason that China's universe had expanded. The past had a competitor. All the new questions arose. Was something to be valued because it was Chinese? Or would any Chinese something have to be measured thenceforth against a Western something? What shall we think of our Confucian tradition? No one had asked this before. Should it remain because it remains the best way forward (which, after all, was the reason it became the tradition)? Or should it remain because it is Chinese? The latter was a very different thought: The tradition should remain because it had so long remained.

This last matter became controversial. The axis of the debate after the Opium Wars turned approximately on what we can call the Lampedusa thesis. There was no question of the validity of the Confucian tradition—not yet. The question became how to build walls around it. Conservatives asserted that alternatives presented by the West should be rejected so that China could go on being China and the present filled to its brim with the past and precedent. The West was Western—enough to turn it away. Then there were the "self-strengtheners," as they called themselves. These argued as young Tancredi in Lampedusa's novel argues with his uncle: Let us adopt foreign things and so keep the core of ourselves intact.

Before the Qing collapsed in 1911, reformers were to make many efforts to save it. Modernize the bureaucracy, the army, the schools; build a railway system; experiment with foreign institutions—all this and more, they urged. This was the time of Kang Youwei, the noted reformer mentioned earlier. China could make itself modern and still be Chinese, Kang argued. The Qing could get it done. Kang, like many others, was taken up with numerous matters of policy and method, notably during a period in 1898 called the Hundred Days' Reforms, a late effort to keep the emperor on the throne.

But all in the name of what? What was the driving idea? We cannot be surprised to find that it came from the past—not the recent past, even, but the deep past, the past of the great metaphysical thinkers.

THE TERMS OF THE DISCOURSE came down from a Song dynasty philosopher named Zhu Xi, a twelfth-century interpreter of Confucius. Zhu (Chu Hsi in the old spelling) remains an influential figure in the history of Chinese thought. All that makes up the universe, Zhu said, is composed of *li* and *qi*. *Li* is principle, the law of things, the immutable ideal. *Qi* is manifestation, physical matter, form, the earthly deeds of men. There was knowledge, to put it another way, and there was actualization. All things had both *li* and *qi*, but the former—and once again we are not surprised—was privileged. *Li* is innately good; *qi* must be properly husbanded, for the *qi* of things is mutable, which leaves it susceptible to corruption, misjudgment, and human foible.

Zhu's thought engendered many critics and commentators, beginning among his contemporaries and extending down to Fung Youlan, the twentieth-century philosopher. But the critical moment came in the decades after the Opium Wars. This was when the self-strengtheners formulated their new idea for China: There was *ti*, and there was *yong*. *Ti* was essence, substance; *yong* was function, application, the doing of things. *Ti*, like the *li* of Zhu Xi's teaching, was the privileged value; *yong* was necessary but merely useful.

The point was best made by a Confucian reformer named Zhang Zhidong, an imperial viceroy with an enthusiasm for railroads and smokestack industries. Zhang imported China's first steel mill from England, every piece of it, and put it into production in 1894—a disaster, as it turned out, for Zhang took no account of where the ore would come from and where the coal deposits lay. "Chinese learning for fundamental principles," Zhang's most famous slogan went, "Western learning for practical application." This was "*ti* and *yong*" as clearly stated as it ever would be. Zhang elaborated the thought in a work later translated as *China's Only Hope:*

> If the Chinese heart throbs in unison with the heart of the sages, expressing the truth in irreprovable conduct, in filial piety, brotherly love, honesty, integrity, virtue; if government is loyalty and protection, then let government make use of foreign machinery and the railway from morning to night, and nothing untoward will befall the disciples of Confucius.

It was in this fashion that Tokyo and Beijing, the capitals of the Confucian world, sought to navigate into the modern era. And it is interesting to reflect upon whether the concepts of *li* and *qi*, in their nineteenth-century iteration, were not the last things Japan ever learned from the Chinese. *Ti* and *yong*, spirit and things: They were not quite congruent, but there seems no denying their proximity. They both rested on the same tradition. The nineteenth century marked a momentous turn because *ti* (spirit) and *yong* (things) would thenceforth be considered separately.

Certain purposes were served. One could partake of the vulgar things the Westerners brought and still proclaim the valor of the spirit, that which made one Chinese or Japanese. The old would be transported forward. One could preserve while also absorbing—indeed, one absorbed in the name of preservation. Humiliation was avoided. And there came into being a phenomenon that has long driven Westerners to the edge of misunderstanding and then, usually, over it. This was the paradox of "great change amid no change" and, compounding matters further, the possibility of the inverse: "no change amid great change."

Problems developed, as already suggested. The old learning— the *ti* of things, to stay with the Chinese terms—had been *ti* because it served. Now it was *ti* only because it was *ti* and because *ti*, a spirit, was needed in the face of all the *yong* coming across the ocean. *Ti*, in this way, would work no longer.

In Japan's case, the Meiji modernization had not been completed before the Japanese were losing themselves to that evanescent thrill of material consumption—"the fierce joys of a time-devouring locomotion," as Kakuzo Okakura put it. The crisis runs all through the mid- and late-Meiji literature. Long before the Japanese spirit took its tragic stand in the Pacific war, its posture was implicitly defensive. It had acquired that self-consciousness that betrayed its fate as failure. Postwar Japan is not difficult to describe. The defeat in 1945 being essentially one of values, it was *ti* that collapsed, and *yong* simply became the new *ti*: Things themselves became the new ideal. At the other end of the line, in the late 1980s, when Japan was at last rich and the *ti* of the postwar period was realized, one of our better Japan scholars put a name to it: the emptiness of Japanese affluence.

CHINA'S STORY HAS been more complex. What followed the Qing abdication in early 1912 was a long period of unrest and the blooming of many flowers: warlords, republicans, reformers, revolutionaries. All the questions already suggested— "Chineseness," the national direction, the place of tradition, what to do about the West—coalesced in the May Fourth Movement, a student uprising that erupted in 1919. May Fourth was vigorously modern, vigorously anti-Confucian. Its legacy has been long-lived. The Tian'anmen incident seventy years later was explicitly an echo of "the May Fourth spirit."

Among the interesting creations to come out of the May

Fourth era were a pair called Mr. Science and Mr. Democracy. They were conjured from the ferment early in 1919—with none of the satire Westerners might assume—by a theorist named Chen Duxiu. "Only these two gentlemen," Chen wrote, "can save China from the political, moral, academic, and intellectual darkness in which it finds itself." This was an important remark. It was to declare a new *ti*—one rooted not in nostalgia for China as it had been but in China as it was, as it had become.

Mr. Science and Mr. Democracy have traveled far. A statue commemorating them stands today on the campus of Beijing University, where Chen was a lecturer (the young Mao having been among his students). The curious things to note about this odd-sounding couple are two. They betoken a certain instrumentality at the core of Chinese thinking; Chen, indeed, was an avowed utilitarian. Science and democracy were now to be declared the path ahead, but they seemed in some measure to be conceived of as commodities—something that might arrive on the docks at Dalian, in crates. Equally, Mr. Science and Mr. Democracy portended something key in twentieth-century China: The *ti* of the Confucian tradition was losing its attraction. By the 1920s the very old thing that must be preserved was fading. Mr. Science and Mr. Democracy stepped forward to suggest that another *ti*, from another place, an un-Chinese place, might stand where the tradition once stood.

Mr. Science and Mr. Democracy were much discussed in the decades after May Fourth. And Mr. Science has never faltered as a figure in modern China. His counterpart has had a different fate. Mr. Democracy is nominally honored; nothing is ever done in modern China but in the name of democracy. But in practice Chen's creation, plainly enough, fell out of step. This was Mao's deed.

We cannot reduce the Helmsman's time to a few sentences. Fifty-five years passed between the founding of the Communist

Party in a small room in Shanghai, two years after the May Fourth events, and Mao's death in 1976. But for our purpose his rise represented the declaration of a new *ti*. The old tradition was stamped out. The new tradition was socialism—the new *ti*. It was not, as Malraux put it in *Man's Fate*, simply a matter of will. It was the idea that would enable China to escape the grip of the past and instantly fill the void left in its belief system.

Socialism was an import. It came from the West, but it was critical of the West. It was the topmost flower of Western tradition—the logical outcome of the Enlightenment, as Edmund Wilson traced the line in *To the Finland Station*. But it stood against what the Western tradition had produced: imperialism, the subjugation of others, and the Opium Wars and other such events. Indians, as we will consider, had a similar taste for the self-critical West—the alternative West, as some Indians like to call it. Another kind of Middle Kingdom would be achieved. China could restore its greatness—the Maoist dream—but it would match Western power with power of another kind, and it would make no apologies: Despicable imperialists could still be despicable imperialists. China would rise above the old hurts with the gleaming smiles and apple-y cheeks pictured in propaganda posters, but it would join the victimizers' critics, not the victimizers.

The past was similarly complicated. History's tyranny, as a noted Sinologist named it, was supposedly overcome. During the Cultural Revolution, Mao swept up and made to discard the Confucian tradition among "the four olds"—old culture, old thinking, old habits, old customs. But the tradition did not disappear—or, rather, it disappeared only from view. The past remained as an instrument of manipulation. Tradition was to be excoriated in public life, but it was there in every Chinese— "the edifice within"—to be called upon when useful. Mao was vehemently anti-Confucian; Mao was profoundly Confucian;

China had left behind the tradition; China continued to live by the tradition: There is something in all four of these to be defended.

There would be more to come in the matter of *ti* and *yong*. Socialism, as anyone who has looked at China without ideological blinders must acknowledge, did much to make China modern—notably, though not only, in advancing the place and prerogatives of women. As the new *ti*, however, its life proved limited. Mr. Democracy had dropped from sight, but he was not deceased.

THERE IS NOTHING particularly Asian about the impulse to defend one's way of being from invasive influences. Xenophobia is commonly assigned as an Asian attribute, and this is fair as far as it goes. We do not need to elaborate on the anti-foreignism evident at various moments in Japan, China, and elsewhere in Asia. But this must be seen as a consequence of history, nothing more. And there was much to be phobic about, it is also fair to point out. It is doubtful anyone else would have responded much differently.

To distinguish between the instrumental and that held to be of higher value: Neither was this a habit unique to Asians. For all the early talk of lowly legs and feet, this distinction was part of what Asia began to import along with all the *yong* that came from the West. Rationalization was an Enlightenment ideal. Max Weber, the German sociologist, explored the fragmentation of reason and the elevation of science at length in the nineteenth century. With progress of this kind, Weber warned, we enter "the iron cage" of formal rationality. But the making of this distinction in Asia, the entering into the cage, had particular consequences. It inhibited the development of individual subjectivity: Asians would "modernize" but not "become modern." For better or worse (as we will consider later), they continued to conceive of human existence as fundamentally a participation in a unity, a oneness. Equally, *ti* and *yong* became the scaffolding within which Asians developed the practice of doubling. The distinction was ready-made for the ennobling of the spirit and so for the fertilization of weakness, nostalgia, and *ressentiment* as habits of mind.

Could China and Japan have managed the nineteenth-century encounter other than they did? Was there an alternative to the fraught, consequential error of attempting an Eastern *ti* and a Western *yong*? We can address this now, but only from our own position. A good deal of experience and thinking resides with us, and nineteenth-century Asians were not so equipped. They had no way of measuring collective preferences and no means to calculate the possibilities that lay in them. They had no tradition of self-reflection as this arose in the modern era. In consequence, certain fundamental misapprehensions are now evident.

Foremost among these is the very idea of the modern. China and Japan mistook this to involve the material alone, what they could see, and so neglected all that produced material superiority. They missed, we can say, the *ti* of the West. We must now elaborate on the distinction between "modernization" and "being modern." The former involves technological advance, industry, production, and material progress altogether; the latter is a question of psychology, of consciousness, of the individual's capacity to exercise his or her reason freely. It is a question, in short, of the cultivation of a modern self, from which arises modern relations with others. Zhang Zhidong's ill-fated steel mill is emblem enough of the difference between the two. It was the work of a modernizer, not of a modern man.

Neither did Asia's Confucians grasp the question of time—or they understood it differently, at least. With all the *yong* that arrived in crates on docks and in how-to manuals (which still flood Asian bookshops), there came a Western conception of chronology: The Westerners are up there, ahead, in the "now" of the universe; their time is clock-time, a commodity. We are back here, behind, in the "once-was," in village time. The implanting of this perception was as powerful as any cannon made of British brass.

There was also the related assumption that time is homogeneous. Either one was modern, or one was what came before. So one doubled: One put on a Western suit and was modern or one wore a kimono and was traditional, but one could not dress in kimono and be modern. Okakura was interesting in this respect. He often, and pointedly, dressed in kimono during his residence in Boston. It must have been a way of rejecting the act of doubling. By the end of his life he took a militant view of the tea ceremony: To practice it was an act of defiance against all that would discredit it. So could the observance of tradition be invested with a certain aspect of resistance.

THE EVENTS OF THE nineteenth century, the threads that run through Asian thought, may be interesting enough in themselves. But we take them up because the consequences lie before us. Asia still wrestles with them. Spirit and things, *ti* and *yong*, were the start of something, a journey into the modern, and the completion of absolutely nothing. Jiwei Ci, a Chinese scholar of the Tian'anmen generation and an exceptional observer of his country, put it well in his reflections on the events that marked his formative years—the Tian'anmen protests and China's prevalent preoccupation afterward with "hedonism," meaning material prosperity alone: "The disjunction of human activity into ends and means, pure intention and mere activity, self-sufficient value and subservient instrumentality, is a symptom of a profound cultural crisis, not its solution."

This crisis and its aftermath are a defining feature of Asia as it is. It is only now that resolution presents itself, which is what makes our time as interesting and moving as the starting point, a century and a half and more after the crisis began.

One of Edward Said's later essays, published posthumously in the book called *On Late Style*, concerns Jean Genet and his ties to Palestinians, but part of it bears upon our topic. It consists of several apparently contradictory thoughts. "Identity is what we impose on ourselves," the passage begins, "through our lives as social, historical, political, and even spiritual beings." And then this, further in the same paragraph:

> Identity is the process by which the stronger culture, and the more developed society, imposes itself violently upon those who, by the same identity process, are decreed to be a lesser people.

And then the finish, the summation:

> Imperialism is the export of identity.

None of these assertions cancels any other. In the balance of them lies the question of human agency.

We have spent some time on what Japan and China did in response to the West, and not much time on what the West did. This is not to re-reckon the books on the imperial era. It is to attempt a shift in perspective so that we might see Asia more fully. Asians were the "done to" in the century that belonged to someone else, on the receiving end of the modern. This does not require us to cast them, Arnold-like, as passive victims with lowered heads, no history, and no decisions to make. Hardly were they passive, they faced overmany decisions, and their history had practically everything to do with the choices they made. If we do not understand this, we will never grasp the new possibilities that lie before Asia in the new century.

Identity is what we impose on ourselves . . . Identity is imposed by the stronger on the weaker . . . Identity is an export. That makes three truths. The West made Asia as it is by way of its material superiority. Asia made Asia by what it had already been thinking and then what it thought and did in response to the arriving West. Every export involves an import, however complex, messy, and unbalanced the transaction and the terms of trade.

OF TOKYO'S MANY CURIOUS QUARTERS, so many with not-always-evident stories to tell about themselves, Akihabara is surely singular. It is, in a phrase that suits the place entirely, the Japanese capital of things.

Akihabara used to be a plain neighborhood—shabby, functional in the way postwar Japan remade itself. It was where you went to find electronics of any variety. There were shops that sold computers, televisions, tape recorders, music systems; and there were hundreds of others, floor upon floor of them in cheaply constructed commercial buildings, that sold hard-to-find gadgets and parts of things. The place was paradise for those among us known as geeks. But there was nothing else.

Akiba, as the district is commonly known, has changed over the years. The shops remain, but gradually in the 1990s, and then more swiftly after the turn of our century, Akiba became the center of Japanese youth culture, or a certain strand of it. Apart from the computer shops, there are computer game parlors in which people spend many hours and many hundreds of dollars. Video games are nearly countless. There are also huge shops for people who collect toys—plastic models of characters in *manga* comics or television series or films. Someone will pay six thousand or seven thousand dollars for a model of a robot or a monster because there were only a few dozen made. Next to it will be another one just like it but at half the price.

"Why?" I once asked a clerk as I studied a pair of such things.

"This one has a small crack in the enamel on the back of the left foot. See? Look, just there."

I looked and saw, but with difficulty.

Out on the street there is the phenomenon known as the maids' café. These are places where girls dress in the black and white of a Western maid, the kind that appeared in old Hollywood films. They move in robotic fashion, a little in the manner of puppets. Lolitas move this way, too: These are girls dressed in imitation of the ingenue in Nabokov's novel; somehow the story made it into the minds of Japanese young people and there took root. Maids and Lolitas remain in character at all times. They never surrender the artifice, like the British performance artists Gilbert and George.

Some of this may seem familiar. But when you stand at the heart of the place that originated this idea of culture, if that is the word, certain aspects of it become clear. There is the totalized artificiality of the environment. A game center is an assault of noise and light sealed within strange-colored walls with no windows. Things are furtive in Akiba. No one will give you his or her real name. One cannot take pictures in the shops selling models and toys—there are signs prohibiting it. There is also a peculiar solitude: Thousands of people milling and looking and playing and buying, each one lost in a search for this or that. Related to the solitude is the cultivation of obsession. Without obsession there would be no Akiba.

AKIHABARA IS A WINDOW onto something interesting that has taken place since the late 1980s, when the Japanese caught up to the West. It is one of the centers, if not the center, for people known as *otaku*. Like the things they spend their time on— *manga*, animated film, computer games, costumes—the term may be familiar, for it has traveled far outside of Japan. But again, to look at the *otaku* in the society that has given rise to them—this will tell us something about Japan (and Asia) and the East's journey into the modern.

Otaku is a second-person pronoun: It means "you," but "you" in a particular way. It was originally an honorific reserved for those of another family or *ie,* an extended household. This implies distance—households by tradition being closed to outsiders. So in the term itself we find suggestions of an odd conservatism and nostalgia and of fated isolation and unbridgeable gulfs, one person from another. *Otaku,* indeed, form families and households somewhat in the old way on the basis of shared obsessions. And when belonging of this kind becomes the basis of identity, there is no public space; strangers remain forever strangers.

Otaku took on its current meaning in the mid-1980s. It was then that groups of young people—alienated, solipsistic, dysfunctional, plainly a symptom of a malady in Japanese life—began to form around pointless (pointedly pointless) obsessions. One could not miss the extent to which these obsessions served to shut the rest of the world out, forming a psychological enclosure. In the early days the obsessions of *otaku* were notably recherché. Train schedules were a common example: An *otaku* would dedicate his waking hours to studying the departure time of every train between, say, Tokyo or Osaka and some obscure town on the other side of Japan, when and where it stopped, how long it stayed in each station, when it arrived at the obscure town, how many cars it had, which among them was the dining car, where on the platform the dining car would come to rest at each stop. A typical *otaku* was socially incompetent outside his (usually but not always) circle. And he was incapable of forming relations with women, which I have always found to be among the *otaku*'s most curious characteristics. An *otaku* is an unformed self. He manifests the failure of modernization to allow for the formation of a modern, integrated personality.

No one paid much attention to the *otaku* when they first appeared. Now they number in the millions by most estimates, and their obsessions come in great variety. Psychiatrists have analyzed them in best sellers, and professors offer courses on them. They are big business for publishers, manufacturers of games and electronics, and film producers. Takashi Murakami, the noted artist and designer, elevates *otaku* culture to an aesthetic: At last Japan has something original, something truly Japanese, to offer the world. *Otaku*, in short, has become a style. Its fashions are available in any Tokyo department store.

None of this is surprising. If the *otaku* were first taken to be marginal eccentrics suffering from arrested development, the Japanese now know they are looking at themselves in a mirror. Time and again I have found myself conversing about the phenomenon with a friend or an acquaintance only to find that he (or she, now) is an *otaku*, or has some sense of identity (furtively expressed, once again) with them. And one circle wider than the *otaku* we find the *freeters*, a term also coined in the 1980s. It consists of "free" and *Arbeiter*, the German for "worker," and *freeters* are those who choose as little casual employment as possible over a place in what we used to call Japan Inc. *Freeters* add millions more to Japan's population of the alienated.

The *otaku* eventually reminded me of a passage in Nietzsche, the famous parable of the madman in the marketplace who declares God to be dead. "Are we not plunging continually?" the madman asks. "Backward, sideward, forward, in all directions? Is there still any up or down? Are we not straying as through an infinite nothing? Do we not feel the breath of empty space?" This is the *otaku*. It is possible to over-freight the phenomenon, perhaps. But I find something profound in it. We recognize in the *otaku* and their obsessions—an obsession with obsessions that lack all significance—a logical outcome. It is the end of the story that began with "Japanese spirit, Western things." The spirit, the essence, the ideal, the *ti:* It cannot survive this bifurcation. When means become end, what follows is a surrender to the absence of all meaning, and then an attempt to elevate no-meaning to a meaning in itself. This is why, surely, so many Japanese can look askance at the *otaku* but cannot bring themselves to any sort of detached, critical appraisal.

SOMETHING HAPPENED IN nineteenth-century Asia that we can usefully term "history's trick." Captivated by what they could see, the Japanese (and others) failed to grasp that the modern era had already begun to exhibit fundamental problems in the West. A crisis was forming beneath the surface—the crisis of disenchantment. This would soon prove to be implicit in the modern condition. The idea of progress, the subjective individual, the culture of materialism, secularism as an imperative, the nation-state as it had by then evolved—all this was beginning to show signs of weakness, flaws. When Weber wrote of the iron cage, he meant in part the loss of any prospect of transcendence. The West's belief in the meaning of material things, for all its outward confidence, was already starting to collapse from within. Asia missed this. It accepted all that was modern at face value, uncritically. Self-doubt, internal decay, the thought of an exhausted paradigm: Only those Western artists and thinkers on the forward edge of things spoke of such matters, and Asia did not hear them.

Famously enough, it was Nietzsche who named this condition in its modern manifestation. This is what his madman describes when he talks about life as a directionless plunge. This is Nietzsche's nihilism. In its Asian iteration I have come to call it "consumerist nihilism" to underscore the essential role of things, material possessions, in perpetuating it.

Nihilism of this kind produces a distinct effect among Asians. I have named it "the bittersweet smile." With modernization came the surprise of emptiness, so we can describe the bittersweet smile by way of a set of negatives. There is no ideal, no belief, no memory, no transcendence. There is activity without vitality. There is no sense, above all, of a new beginning, as modernization seemed to promise—only the logical conclusion of past errors, a future that is nothing more than an extension of the present. This is the bittersweet smile—the smile of the *otaku*, among many others.

Of all the things Asians have taken from the West—borrowed, imitated, absorbed, learned from manuals—it is nihilism that appears to trouble them most. It was upon them before they understood it, and it is the import that sits most awkwardly among them. At the same time, consumerist nihilism is considerable among Japan's exports in the early twenty-first century. Americans buy it back—by way of *otaku* culture, for instance—just as they gave Japan auto technology and then came to prefer Japanese cars. Many Asians buy it, too: They are still learning from those who first mastered Western things—if, indeed, things did not come to master them.

MANY SCHOLARS NOW STUDY Japan's diffusion of its popular culture across Asia. But there is little that is new in this pattern. To understand it, we must cast it against Asia's modern history—a century and some of experience.

As China struggled to find its way after the Opium Wars, it seemed apparent at the Qing court and among the intellectuals that Japan had a formula that worked. Japan had been China's student, the Middle Kingdom's periphery, for nearly two millennia, but with the coming of the West the student became the teacher. Two events brought this home to the Chinese: Japan's victory in the Sino-Japanese War of 1894–95 and its triumph over Russia a decade later. Japan became a magnet for the Chinese in this period. The treaty that settled the Sino-Japanese War was as bitter and humiliating as anything the Qing ever signed with Westerners, but thousands of mainland students soon flocked to Japanese universities to grasp what it was the Japanese had done. Lu Xun, the great writer of twentieth-century China, studied in Tokyo. Sun Yat-sen made Japan his base for a time. Kang Youwei, the monarchist reformer of the late-Qing period, drew inspiration from the Japanese. They had modernized and kept their emperor: Could China not do the same?

The Chinese studied others, of course, but the Japanese held a special attraction. They were the first to prove, or so it seemed, that one did not have to be Western to be modern. In this way the Japanese seemed to turn the whole of the Enlightenment tradition on its head. "To progress you must be like us," Europeans had been saying since the eighteenth century. Now the Japanese were saying something different. It comes to a single word: Japan made the modern accessible. It became a place in between; it softened the shock of Western things.

The ambivalence in relations between Japan and its neighbors since this period differs now only in order of magnitude. Japan made the twentieth century a catastrophe for the rest of Asia as it pursued an empire of its own. And this makes for startling anomalies. In 2005, Chinese students spent two weeks attacking Japanese places and things—the embassy in Beijing, the consulate in Shanghai, Japanese cars and shops—to protest a new Japanese textbook with yet another questionable account of "the Fifteen-Year War," as conscientious Japanese term the conflict that ended in 1945. But at any moment one can find Chinese consuming Japanese products, playing Japanese computer games, or taking instruction in the modern by way of new television dramas from across the East China Sea. Fascinating it is, many Chinese will tell you, that the Japanese actually lived with Westerners during the seven years of the Occupation. How well they must know the Occident's ways.

IT IS WELL KNOWN, at least among Asians, that 1964 was another triumph for the Japanese. Nineteen years after the surrender, Japan was formally welcomed into the OECD, the club of advanced nations. A lot less abstractly, for those who owned television sets, Japan became that year the first non-Western nation to host the Olympics. Japanese athletes won sixteen gold medals at the summer games in Tokyo, where a not-much-used stadium still marks the site. The gold that meant most went to the women's volleyball team. It defeated the Soviets, and history produced another of its ironies. It was the second time in the century Japan had turned back the Russians. Faintly but unmistakably, the volleyball victory seemed freighted with some of the same symbolism the world had invested in the Russo-Japanese War: Japan was arriving among "the powers" once again.

At the time of the Tokyo Olympics, Japanese television was also broadcasting something else that would soon capture imaginations beyond the islands. *Astro Boy* began as a *manga* in the early 1950s, when the Japanese were still living under the American Occupation. Its creator, Osamu Tezuka, was an admirer of Walt Disney, and his comic eventually had numerous iterations on television and in movie theaters. These continue today. Weirdly enough, Tokyo declared the title character a kind of goodwill ambassador in 2007.

From *Astro Boy* has grown the immense universe of anime, animated film. And from anime has grown a yet more immense industry built upon Japan's export of what are called cultural products. South Korea and Taiwan have lifted old bans they once had on cultural imports from Japan; China bought its first anime production not long after Deng Xiaoping opened China in 1978. They are all markets for Japanese products now, and so is the rest of Asia. *Manga*, television, film, video, computer disks, fashion: This is one way Japan projects "soft power"—not only in Asia, but notably in Asia. "We have a grasp on the hearts of young people in many countries," Taro Aso, who recently did a turn as Japan's prime minister, once said. "Not the least of these is China."

In the 1990s, with its reforms well under way, China became a large market for a certain genre of Japanese television productions called trendy dramas. For a long time these circulated by way of pirated computer disks that served an apparently bottomless market. The settings of these things—no small part of the point—varied even less than the plots. A boy and a girl both live in immaculately contemporary Tokyo apartments. There are expensive clothes, German cars, candlelit dinners, bottles of French wine left casually on kitchen counters. We must also note what is absent. There is no clutter of any kind. There are no traditional clothes. And there are no families—never a trace of extended households, filial obligations, aging uncles, or any of the old, familiar fetters. At the height of the piracy craze, the mainland's illegal market for Japanese trendy dramas was estimated (by the industry, admittedly) at more than three billion disks, worth eighteen billion dollars were they sold legally.

The Chinese cracked down on piracy only when mainland producers were able to make their own trendy dramas. These turned out to be replicas of the Japanese products in all but locale: They were typically set in Shanghai. I once watched several episodes of a Chinese-made trendy drama on a bus from Chengdu to Chongqing. And there it all was: handsome advertising exec, long-legged film actress, a Porsche, a duplex, a crystal vase in the entrance foyer. It was jarring. On the screen at the front of the bus, China as it aspires to be; out the window, China as it is—dusty, struggling, plainly dressed, goldtoothed, workaday China.

How to live, how to work, how to love in the modern way, how to spend money, how to dress, how to move one's body, how to look casual while driving a costly car, how to drink a glass of wine: The programs emanating or copied from Japan are dense with semiology. They are instruction manuals for those desiring to become modern and absorb Western things and ways. For all such lessons, Japan is the place to look— "foreign," as a Chinese friend once explained, "but not so foreign."

GUANGZHOU, WHICH WESTERNERS used to call Canton, has little of the old, worn elegance of Shanghai. In the latter city, famously enough, East and West met in the early years of Modernism and produced something that was not quite either one: It was both, and we now call this Shanghai Modern. Guangzhou had no such stylish phase. It has always been the grittier city.

But Guangzhou is a window nonetheless. It is where China connected with the West in the eighteenth century, and something of the legacy remains. If it is arriving in China—a product, a fashion, a new trend in this or that—it often arrives in Guangzhou first. One can see where China is going and what it proposes to be because one can still see where China—poor, striving China, without Shanghai's veneer—has been. It was in Guangzhou in 1961 that Deng Xiaoping made his famous remark about cats—black or white made no difference so long as the mouse got caught. Three decades later Deng took his final bow on a tour of Guangzhou and a few rising cities nearby. "To get rich is glorious," he is said to have proclaimed, although it seems he may not have made the point in quite those words.

I knew a filmmaker in Guangzhou named Du Gang. His father had been an army man sent south from Beijing, so Du was and was not part of the city—a local and an outsider both. He was thirty-three when I met him, on the terrace of a restaurant at the edge of the Pearl River, and he was just finishing a script. It consisted of numerous episodes, separate but linked. They were filled with the conflicts that are common in the China Deng's reforms have created: successful executives, pregnant lovers and betrayed wives, overbearing families, forgiveness, vengeance, or indifference, the leaving behind of one life to begin another. The last of these episodes came from a friend's experience. A husband and wife are raising a child in an extended family, but the wife envies the neighbors their cars and big houses. They quit their jobs to work for Amway, the marketing company that sells (in addition to its line of products) dreams of entrepreneurship and independence. The small house goes and a big one replaces it, but with the small house went a certain contentedness the couple can no longer find. Yet another kind of nostalgia sets in.

"True story," Du said. "A few years ago they were happy. Now, every time I see them, they're frantically on the telephone to clients. They don't know what they're really looking for."

Du had given up on plots, he said. Story lines, character, narrative thread—none of it was of much use if he was to make films about a nation in frenetic motion. There were only passages, one following another without apparent pattern. "Nobody's very sure," Du once said to me, "what they are supposed to think is worthwhile."

To grasp what they are doing, to become aware of China as it is, to swim in the deep ocean of things—this will emerge as the project of Du's generation. But for now a certain unconsciousness remains prevalent among the Chinese. After I met Du, I decided to explore it as I had in Akihabara from time to time. There was, indeed, something Japanese in Du's episodes and descriptions. The lostness he talked about and tried to put into his films seemed to be Japan's lostness—the inexpressible lostness that had emerged in the 1980s along with the *otaku*.

I once found a maids' café in another section of Guangzhou. It was on a small side street that had already made the conversion, familiar in cities across China, from traditional shophouses to trendy retail spaces. The café's owner was a man in his thirties named Yue Xia. "In Japanese, I'm Tsukisita," he explained as he sat to talk. This was the first maids' café in China, Yue told me in the course of a long conversation, and it was part of the coming thing. He called it ACG, meaning animation, comics, and games.

"It's promising," Yue said with an entrepreneur's enthusiasm.

"The prime time for this is maybe two or three decades away, but I see prospects as a business. Japan in contemporary history invaded many countries, and people are supposed to hate it. But because of ACG it's easy to accept Japanese culture—never mind the invasions."

Yue had not been to Japan much—one brief visit, he said, and I wondered if he had made even that—but he had thought things through. The imagery of anime and the café and all the rest were originally Western, but Japan had transformed them. And now Japan was simply giving back to Asia just as it had once taken from Asia. In time Yue reminded me of Kakuzo Okakura, the fin de siècle aesthete who had imagined Asia as one and Japan as the gatherer and museum keeper of its past. Now it seemed the keeper of Asia's future.

I decided to ask Yue about the fatalism I found at the core of *otaku* culture and why young Chinese now seemed so eager to import this as well.

"People say the *otaku* reject the world or something," Yue replied. "This is a misconception. ACG is modern art. It's a moneymaking business. It's not something you disrespect. It shows that *otaku* can also contribute to society."

It seemed a long way, at that moment, from Akihabara and obsessions with train schedules. From Japan, along with all the method, the technique, the *yong*, China now takes its nihilism, too. So does history's trick echo on. And it afflicts many, as Du Gang wanted to capture in his films and as any traveler on the mainland can discover. But before it is finished with all its afflicting, the nihilism of consumption will be a business opportunity: nihilism as pure style, as product.

Ti AND *YONG*, SPIRIT AND THINGS: The fate of these ways of ordering the world is a frame through which to understand many complex events. From the Opium Wars to Commodore Perry to Japan's famous victories at the turn of the twentieth century to the Chinese revolution and the excesses of the Maoist era, and now to the post-Maoist reforms: An incessant alternation between the ideal and the power of things drove East Asia through all of these moments.

In Japan the tension between spirit and things built up over three-quarters of a century and went slack in an instant on the morning of August 15, 1945. And by way of *ti* and *yong* we can understand much that was said during the Communist era in China and much that has been said since. All the slogans of the period, so often odd to the Western sensibility, begin to fall approximately into place.

"Put politics in command," Mao famously exhorted. It was a cornerstone of his thinking. The Cultural Revolution brought the idea to its logical (or illogical) extreme. "Seek truth from facts." This became Deng's counter-command once he was restored to prominence. "Practice is the only test of truth"— this was another of Deng's favorites. And there was his thought about cats and mice, of course.

In the background of these contending views—so momentous in twentieth-century China, so costly in human lives, so determining of China's fate—seems to lie the discourse of *ti* and *yong*. "Politics in command" was a defense of essence. The means must conform to it. In the twelfth-century terms of Zhu Xi, Mao would have to stand on the side of the old concept of *li*. Deng, of course, was all about *yong*—*qi*, in the Song dynasty terminology. He found his intellectual ancestors among Qing dynasty thinkers of a school known as Evidential Learning. Scholarly introspection would not do, they argued: The habit had weakened the Ming to the point of collapse. What we can see is what matters.

Language was of immense importance during the Chinese revolution. Words betokened systems of thought. Mao stood

for belief, in simple terms. Deng stood for nothing-to-believe-
in. Deng won the day after many centuries. He did so delicately, for Mao's legacy is more compelling among the Chinese
than most outsiders presume. After a century of degradation,
he famously got China to "stand up"—that telling phrase from
the 1950s—and believe in something. This counts, in memory,
more than Mao's many messes. This is why Deng and his
cohort came up with that notion we know familiarly today:
socialism with Chinese characteristics. It is another way for
China to say what it cannot truly admit: When *yong* became *ti*,
there was no longer any *ti*; life is all method and things.

I knew a young Chinese named Wang Shuo who was practicing the still-arcane craft of business journalism in Beijing.
He once asked me, "Do you think China now is like Japan in
the '80s?"

We were sharing a taxi through the capital late one evening
after a long dinner at a friend's apartment not far from Tian'anmen Square. All around us as we peeled along an elevated
expressway the lights of the new Beijing twinkled. Beneath
were miles of crumbling Communist-era apartment buildings
and here and there a row of surviving *hutong* houses.

I thought about Wang's question.

"Not Japan in the 1980s," I replied. "Japan in the 1880s."

It is roughly right. The only other comparison might be
Japan in the 1950s, the time of Kitakyushu's rise. For Deng and
those who have come after him, as for the Meiji modernizers
and then the postwar rebuilders, the imperative has been to
make anew all that can be seen. And part of the underlying
desire is to show, to appear—meaning the drive is to measure
up in the eyes of others. It accounts for many things. Social
inequities, imbalances between city and village, environmental
carelessness—this was Japan "then," and Japan's "then" is precisely China's "now." The only difference is how much more
quickly things now unfold. We can already talk of the empti-

ness of Chinese affluence, even as most of the country has yet to achieve any such condition.

ONE AFTERNOON AT Uncle Wang's teahouse I began planning a visit to Dalian, the coastal city famous for its destroy-it-and-guess mayor. I wanted to see what remained of the layers of history—Russian, Japanese, Chinese Nationalist, Chinese Communist—and what had become of the port now that the cities it had served have turned into China's rust belt.

"Dalian," Wang said. "You'll have to meet my old school-mate Sun."

Sun Guowei, sixtyish as Wang was, turned out to be as welcoming as Wang had promised. We were staying, a colleague and I, at a hotel on Renmin Lu—People's Road—and Sun picked us up for lunch. He was silver haired and wore a well-cut tweed jacket. He drove us in an elegant Japanese car to his favorite seafood restaurant.

The dishes, as so often when one is a guest in China, arrived and arrived beyond our capacity to consume them. I was especially fond of the beer—the palest, freshest lager I had ever drunk, in color somewhere between springwater and a light white wine.

"Chinese technology," Sun explained, "and our water. When Bo was mayor, he changed the flow of rivers. We got the best water."

Sun was an amateur historian, it turned out. He told us about Dalian as it had been—a town of small grease-and-oil industries—and as it aspired to be: a passenger port in northeast Asia and a center for advanced technology. Sun's own story ran all through this. He had started as an assembly-line worker in a television plant and had worked his way up to head the export department. Then came the reforms, and Comrade Sun began his own business. When I met him, he was producing cables and other bits of hardware for Internet systems. And he was rich. His son had recently returned from studies in England. He had come home with excellent English and would someday take over the business.

After lunch we drove south toward Lushun, site of Japan's decisive battle with the Russians a century earlier. Along the way we passed through many miles of countryside—scrubby slopes on one side, the sea on the other.

Sun explained, "This will be Dalian's Silicon Valley. That's the developers' idea."

It seemed halfway done already. Everywhere, something new was pushing aside something old. There were decrepit villages with no electricity or plumbing, and next to them office buildings with the names of Japanese and American corporations on them. Then a gated community of villas, or a shopping mall, then another village, then a herd of grazing goats.

Afternoon turned to dusk, and Sun would take us to dinner. It was a special place, he said—better, even, than the seafood restaurant in the city. It turned out to be a plaster-walled house at the edge of one of the old villages. It had a dirt floor, and we ate in the style peasants had for centuries during the cold seasons: on a raised platform with worn cushions around us and a smoldering fire beneath to give heat.

Another side of Sun came out as we ate our fatty pork and overcooked vegetables and drank our warm bottles of beer. A nostalgia I had seen no hint of began to color our conversation. It was in part a nostalgia for the old village but also—and not in contradiction precisely—a nostalgia for the Communist years. Yes, he liked Mayor Bo during his nine years of tearing everything down. But something had been lost.

"Can you say what it is?"

At this, Sun turned to Zhuang Xi, my colleague, and began to wonder aloud in Mandarin. "Don't tell him what I'm about to tell you." Then: "Okay, go ahead and tell him." After this Sun spoke for some time.

"We Chinese are not so happy with ourselves as you might

think," he began in an almost confessional tone. "China's going backward, I think. Power, money: When you're driven by the desire for material satisfaction alone, you're going backward. Look at the way I ordered lunch—too much, just to impress you. People would laugh if they saw that.

"High-rises. People are cut off from one another in high-rises. They have 'more' and 'better,' but relations between one and another are ever more distant. Most people in Dalian came from Shandong Province, so there was familiarity. We lived together; we had little, but we shared. We carried coal for one another; we drank in the evenings. That's all gone now—gone with the old neighborhoods.

"We have a saying: 'Ties between friends are as light as water.' It used to mean they are pure, uncontaminated. Now we mean something else. Now it means they are shallow and there is nothing to them."

When Sun had finished, we made quietly to leave. He had shown me—carefully, after giving it thought—the bittersweet smile of contemporary China, the malaise that haunts all the acquiring and spending in the prosperous cities. It is *ti* and *yong* again: One sits, a Westerner, and listens to the regret and nostalgia that come with all the *yong* China takes from the West. There is little—or perhaps too much—to say.

I never saw Sun again. Zhuang Xi telephoned several times when I was planning trips to Dalian. But he always spoke in a subdued tone, she said, and apologized that he was indisposed.

Eventually we mentioned this to Uncle Wang. And then the news came. Some weeks after we had seen Sun and drunk the wine-like lager of Dalian in celebration of past and future, his son had killed himself. I did not know Sun intimately, though he was generous in our exchanges. But the thought of Sun's story, from the television factory to his son's education in England and then to his son's end and his lapse into silence, has never left me.

2

I WAS ONCE DELAYED for many hours in a desert town called Palanpur. Palanpur lies amid the scrubby land of northwest India, not far from the Pakistan border and the salty, seasonal marshes known as the Rann of Kachchh. It was hot, and the monsoons were still to come. I was waiting for the overnight train that passes through Ajmer and Jaipur on the way to Delhi.

One gets used to staring at things in Indian rail stations for the simple reason that the trains are so often late. A loud-speaker, a porter's cart, a public sink with a row of brass spigots: The wholly ordinary sometimes yields a lesson. This does not happen so much in Japan or China. The small truth hidden in the scenery of everyday life seems to be singularly Indian. Perhaps it is because the scenery is so varied, or because there is a lot of waiting to be done in India, or because time in India, as scholars say, is heterogeneous: The present is made not only of "now" but also of "then," the layers of the past that survive and survive. In Allahabad, the city of Nehru spread along the Ganges, horse-drawn traps crowd the avenues: They are the local taxis.

On the platform that afternoon in Palanpur my eye fell upon a cast-iron rack outside the stationmaster's office. It had been painted many times the bright red of emergency equipment. A heavy beam across the middle had hooks, and each hook held a bucket stenciled with the word "FIRE." Above the buckets hung a thick plate, also of cast iron: Strike it and you sounded the alarm. Altogether, the thing was as pure a specimen of Victoriana as I had ever seen in India: sturdy, bluntly utilitarian, a bit overbuilt, practical and impractical all at once.

I studied the old fire buckets for a long time. They seemed to have something to say for themselves and for India. It is common enough for Westerners to take a certain delight in India's antiquated ways and the remnants of the Raj. They provoke a nostalgia for India as it once was and for Westerners as we once were among Indians. But the fire buckets suggested something more—something about the question of spirit and things in India, something about how the India that once was is still India.

HETEROGENEOUS TIME is everywhere in India: the village hut with a satellite dish, the oxcart hauling sugarcane on the expressway, the barefoot man in a torn sarong taking rupees from a cash machine. But the notion is not so simple as any such example suggests. Heterogeneous time implies a different idea of what it means to be modern. Our standard understanding of progress toward the condition of modernity starts with the assumption of sequence. The primitive man forms a tribe, the tribal man becomes a peasant, the peasant a factory worker, and at last we come out in our industrial and postindustrial societies, wherein the tribal man or the peasant is taken to be "underdeveloped"—that is, premodern, waiting his turn.

This is sequential time—Enlightenment time, we may also call it, homogeneous time. It is the very spine of Western thinking. It is the concept of human development the Japanese and the Chinese accepted when their moment came to modernize. Japan and China suddenly understood themselves not as they were but as "late." Today, the central government in Beijing invites us to join in celebrating "the liberation of feudal Tibet from feudal oppression." We may object, but the thought is a Western import, learned from us. To think in this way becomes an act of exclusion, and often enough those excluded participate in the excluding: What we were before was not modern, so it can be sent to the taxidermist but can no longer be made to matter.

India has not progressed in this way. Human development

has not been taken to be sequential so much as contemporaneous. So there is no habit of doubling the personality, as there has been in Japan and China. To put it another way, India has tended to be inclusive rather than exclusive. A barefoot man at a cash machine is entirely a participant, just as he is, in the entity known as modern India. To find cognitive dissonance in an oxcart on an expressway may do in the pages of *National Geographic*, but there is nothing dissonant about it to the Indian sensibility. This is heterogeneous time.

Indians put this thought many different ways. A friend in Ahmedabad, Gandhi's city, calls it "the availability of confusion." In Hyderabad, one of the high-technology metropolises where change is incessant and everywhere, another friend talks of "plural thinking." In Delhi, I knew an executive at a firm called Fabindia, which contracts with village weavers to make stylish textiles and clothing. Her name was Prableen Sabhaney, and she was talkative and savvy. "It's graying out the blacks and whites," she said one afternoon as we planned a trip to Bhuj, a remote town near the Arabian Sea where some of her weavers worked. "You have to get used to managing ambiguity if you're going to know India."

Neither China nor Japan has managed ambiguity well in the modern era. They imported a chronology that did not permit it. In the late nineteenth century, amid all the talk of *ti* and *yong*, the Chinese reinvented two terms. Certain things could be either *yang* or *tu*. *Yang* means "derived from the ocean" and came to designate foreign things: *Yang wawa*, a doll with round eyes and pale skin; *yang huo*, "foreign fire," a match; *yang san*, a Western-style umbrella. *Tu* means "dirt" and would refer to local things. The new connotations were telling: A *yang* thing was modern, fashionable, desirable; a *tu* thing was backward and not much valued. Some of these terms are still in use: *tu bao*, "dirt dumpling," meaning a country hick; *yang jiu*, good foreign whiskey.

India's idea of how to become modern has made a big differ-ence. Simultaneity, contemporaneous development, heteroge-neous time—however we wish to put it—has let India keep its feet planted properly. There has been plenty of talk since the nineteenth century about science, technology, and the given-ness of Indians to the affairs of the spirit. But there was not so much fear and trembling. Culture never became a task, as it did in Japan and China, and there was little debate in the upper reaches comparable with China's concerning *ti* and *yong*. The arrival of the rail line in Palanpur must have changed many things, but it would have been another case of change amid no change. There would have been no rush to tear down all that was there before and reinvent life, just as there is none now. The fire buckets have done for a long time, and they will con-tinue to do.

Before my train arrived, I took some pictures of the buckets. But what later came to interest me most is not in the images. It is the way all the people on the platform ignored the old con-traption. It was their indifference to this thing from the nine-teenth century as it endures into the twenty-first. The only ones to pay any attention were the stray dogs that populated the station (as they do all Indian rail stations). The dogs seemed to take it as given that the old rack of fire buckets was where water could be had.

INDIA HAS PAID A PRICE for its ambiguity and its notion of het-erogeneous time, primarily in the pace of its material progress. This is perfectly plain if you travel between China and India, and in the case of Japan there is little to compare. Advances have come, but slowly. And they have not spread very far or evenly. Not so many miles beyond the newly glamorous cities one is in the eighteenth century, never mind the nineteenth. A little more than a third of Bombay has the benefit of a sewage system; in Dharavi, with a population of seven million the world's largest slum, there is almost no public sewage. There is still a caste that takes care of these things with shovels, brooms, and pots.

How has India avoided the anguished errors of Japan and China as they made themselves modern? Heterogeneous time is one answer. Another, favored by many Indians in "the new India," globalizing India, is that India has not made the common mistakes of modernization simply because so much of it remains un-modern.

But a new kind of change has begun in India. One sensed it in the early 1980s, and it has been ever more evident in the ensuing years. It has to do with velocity. Some critical mass was achieved in the last years of the last century, and that was when one began to talk of "the new India." The turning point came in 1991, when Delhi began to open what had been a closed, clogged economy. All the reforms that followed have pushed India in a westward direction, and their effect resembles a shot of adrenaline. Fire-bucket change became digital, cellular, and cyberspace change. If India were to have an all-at-once moment in the manner of its easterly neighbors, it would have been at this time.

Now we can no longer talk in India of change amid no change or no change amid change. It is a question of change that prompts more change of the most fundamental sort—a change in consciousness. India is becoming a nation of uplifted eyes. People who defined themselves by fate are coming to define themselves by aspiration—what they want to be, not what they were born to be. A consciousness of poverty gives way to a consciousness of deprivation: People with modern things are modern; people without them are not. There is some *yang* and *tu* to India now.

The new kind of change, the speed and spread of it, has prompted a crisis among Indians. Do we live in heterogeneous time or sequential time? The question may sound abstract, even to many Indians, but it defines their dilemma. The embrace of plurality, the acceptance of ambiguity, a chronology of their own devising, an idea of life as full to the brim with "others"—these were what made Indians Indian, and they may now pass into the past. In their essence the reforms that began in the 1990s are the vessels of sequential time. The West, long an influence, is proposed as a model—later than in Japan and China but in the same way. Another chronology arrives. Everything is reduced to the simplest understanding: It is either modern or not-yet-modern.

Indians have the most curious view of Japan I have ever encountered. Barely manageable India, crumbly, about-to-come-apart India, filthy India by its own description, takes a faintly condescending pity on the Japanese· They have much, but they have surrendered themselves for it. Once, at a cocktail reception in Delhi, I ran into a retired diplomat who had served in Tokyo during the early 1960s. His years in Japan were long before mine, so I wondered about his impressions.

The old ambassador, with long silver hair and a long beard, did not hesitate.

"Much to admire, little to love."

That conversation was some years ago. And it is a question now whether India will much longer sustain the ambassador's confidence. His was the voice of the old India—poor but certain of itself, gifted with the capacity to love itself as it was. The new India speaks with more fragility and is not so self-possessed. It nurses a chronic case of China envy—mixed, paradoxically, with the familiar unease: Many Indians, like many Chinese, already wonder as to the lurking emptiness of the affluence they are coming to crave.

Familiar tropes appear. Talk of "Indianness" is everywhere—what is it, is it eternal or imminently to be lost, can it be saved? This is neither more nor less than a latter-day variation on the theme of *ti* and *yong*, spirit and things. Here and there, especially in Bangalore and the other high-technology centers, one finds the bittersweet smile. And with this come the first flecks of nostalgia among Indians for something—an idea of themselves—they seem powerless to keep from slipping from their grasp.

Once in Ahmedabad, I was talking with a scholar named Shiv Visvanathan, and the conversation shifted to the Japanese. Shiv went straight back to all that was occurring around us, the connection being "the strange paradox of modernization," as he put it. Then he made a memorable remark—memorable because it says something, one way or another, about every Asian nation I have known.

"If you measure all things only by the notion of modernity—if 'the modern' and 'the not modern' are all you have—then the moment of celebration is a moment of sadness. The moment of 'success' becomes the moment of defeat."

ANAND BHAWAN, Nehru's ancestral home in Allahabad, is a large Anglo-Indian affair near the confluence of the Ganges and two other rivers—one flowing before one's eyes and the other a mythical river said to run underground. It makes an interesting visit, as does Nehru's residence in Delhi during his years as prime minister. In both you find the artifacts of a simple but thoroughly modern life as it was lived in Nehru's day: heavy black telephones, fluorescent desk lamps, black-and-white pictures of Nasser, Sukarno, Indira, and others. His bookshelves hold a goodly amount of Marx and Lenin.

Nehru, famously enough, was a man of science. In his writing he was ever attentive to the glories of India's past—the Indus civilization, the ancient myths, the spiritual sophistication that elaborated over many centuries. When his father died, the dedicated secularist was photographed taking the traditional dip of Hindus at the confluence of the rivers. But it was science—"the march of technique"—that India had failed to master and must, Nehru admonished. In a passage that brims with affection for Bharat Mata, Mother India, he once recalled, "I was eager and anxious to change her outlook and appearance and give her the garb of modernity."

In the late 1970s the government built a planetarium next to Anand Bhawan. As tokens of technology go, there is something faintly nineteenth century about a planetarium, it must be said. It is a little "old India." But one cannot help thinking the founding father would have approved: on the family property a place where you can measure your weight on the moon; a short distance away, the Ganges and the sacred confluence.

SUBTRACT PROGRESS from the narrative of India's nationalists, Nehru's narrative, and there would be hardly anything left. Progress in its most pristine meaning, as any *citoyen* would have understood it in Enlightenment France, was the very blood of the independence movement and of all the Congress governments that came after the freedom-at-midnight moment.

How, then, did a nation Nehru located not by way of its soil but in its people's souls avoid a profound neurosis as to spirit and things? And how did it remain so long in its heterogeneous time?

To answer these questions, we can identify a value a cast of mind, a stance toward modern life—we find nowhere so palpably as in India. Over many conversations in many places I came to call it "the eccentric tradition." It is rooted in the Raj and in the England of the nineteenth century, but its fate will have everything to do, I believe, with India's fate in the twenty-first.

We may liken the eccentric tradition to the other side of the moon insofar as it offers another way at practically every human endeavor one can think of. India drew upon the self-critical West—"the defeated West," an Indian friend once described it—just as Mao did only much more eclectically. We can also trace this tradition to an Indian critique of the modern that was evident even as China fought the Opium Wars. And the imported fertilized the indigenous by way of the English eccentrics who found places for themselves in the empire's reaches. The list of these people is long and contains many curious figures: scientists, social reformers, artists, preachers, teachers. Gandhi's closest confidant during the years of his ashram in Ahmedabad, Charles Freer Andrews, was an English eccentric; so were many in the circle around Rabindranath Tagore, the Nobelist in literature.

Organic farming, alternative communities, Ayurvedic medicine, Marxian politics, Theosophy, Montessori schools, Gandhian simplicity, Tagore's university in the forest: India made itself a parade for this sort of thing, and it was all strung on the thread of eccentric thinking. As any such list implies, the eccentric tradition gave India not less than its own way into the modern world. It was, among much else, a way to resist and to select. India could resist the temptation of the traps Japan and China set for themselves when they separated an indigenous spirit from imported things. It could avoid history's trick. It could resist the orthodox Western notion of progress: It could write its own definition, taking from the West what it liked but making it Indian. So did independent India become, to take one evident example, a noted exponent of the economic strategy known as import substitution. If it wanted a tractor, it would not buy a Ford or a John Deere from England or America: It would have its own, a Mahindra or a Swaraj— the latter, indeed, named for the Gandhian concept of village autonomy, an eccentric thought in itself by most Western standards.

East met West in the alternative tradition—a feature of it Indians have always valued. "I have become a queer mixture of the East and the West," Nehru once said, "out of place everywhere, at home nowhere." Or at home anywhere, he might have added, for the thought mixes a little of the cosmopolitan's pride with the lament. Nehru, indeed, must have understood the eccentric tradition well. He and those who came after took their socialism from the Fabians—the English socialism of Sidney and Beatrice Webb, Shaw's socialism. Little Nehru did expresses his stance so well as his prominence in the Non-Aligned Movement. Americans, in particular, grew accustomed during the Cold War to dismissing Non-Aligned as a collection of pro-Soviet sycophants. Nothing could be more uselessly simplistic, for at the core of Nehru's politics we find the thought that truly distinguished India—from everybody, but notably from China and Japan. It would come into the modern world sui generis—an original, a copy of no one.

There is an admirable confidence in this ambition. To face the immensity of the West's material accomplishments and say "We will do this our own peculiar, plodding way" is a project no other non-Western nation ever undertook. We must save the English from their modernity, Gandhi declared many times in his speeches and writings. This was India's confidence—the confidence I found in the old ambassador, drawn in large measure from the eccentric tradition.

In 1916, Tagore traveled to Tokyo to deliver some lectures. Expectations were high: The Indian writer had won his Nobel three years earlier, and he was a friend of Kakuzo Okakura, exponent of the "Asia is one" thesis. But Tagore's presentations landed with a thud. Critics reacted with a hostility approaching outrage. The poet from Bengal had conveyed a thought—several, in fact—that the Japanese were simply not ready to hear.

It was in Tokyo that Tagore noted the distinction between modernization and being modern. The latter, which Tagore called modernism, meant "freedom of mind, not slavery of taste." It meant "independence of thought and action, not tute-

lage under European schoolmasters." It meant "science, but
not its wrong application in life." Being modern was a matter of
self-consciousness in the best sense—knowing who one was—
and it belonged to no one. Modernization, by contrast, was
given by one to another and led to nothing more than imitation. Tagore had it in for modernization, plainly, unless it also
went with being modern. "It is like dressing our skeleton with
another man's skin," he told the Japanese.

One of Tagore's Tokyo critics remarked afterward that he
had just heard "the song of a ruined country." But who was
ahead and who behind at that moment in Asia's modern project? Japan was then on its headlong rush to match the West
materially. Apart from a few of its writers, had it yet conceived
of this undertaking as one requiring the construction of new
selves, new coordinates for the individual personality, along
with new buildings, bridges, and factories? Is the reinvention of
the modern self not the very endeavor much of Asia now
embarks upon? Did India, then, not enjoy a jump on its easterly
neighbors of roughly a century in this respect?

As Tagore implied, the preoccupation with self and subjectivity led to a different relationship between spirit and things.
Kant had argued in the eighteenth century that the two could
not be separated. India understood this: It was one of the
eccentric tradition's fruits. This was the meaning—or one, in
any case—of Gandhi's spinning wheel and his concept of
swaraj, the self-sustaining village: In the things we have made
do we find ourselves; the village is the vessel of the Indian spirit.

Another concept Indians associate with the Gandhian ethos
is called *jugaad*. It means improvising with objects, making do
with what one has, putting old things to new uses. In Delhi
there was an apartment building with an umbrella wired to
work as a satellite dish. There is a project called Goonj whose
work is turning discarded clothing into safe sanitary napkins for
use in poor villages. In Benares, city of silks, I once met a

weaver's wife who was winding thread onto spools with an inverted bicycle, a pedal serving as her handle. This is *jugaad*.

The best-known examples of it are called, indeed, *jugaadi*. They are tractor-like trucks or truck-like tractors—you cannot say which—and no corporation makes them. The motor at the front is made to pump well water, the seat and the steering gear come from either a truck or a motorcycle, and behind there is what Americans would long ago have called a buckboard—a platform made of planks. *Jugaadi* are everywhere. You see these singular things carrying sacks of rice, chaff, cane, furniture, wedding parties, too many farmworkers. They are made, each one, in village workshops.

Most Indians love their notion of *jugaad*. They are as fascinated as any visitor by the things it brings forth. But I have never met an Indian who can explain this affection, which quickly meant to me that the answer was bound to be interesting and must be sought.

In a fishing port on the Arabian Sea called Veraval I finally came upon the *jugaad* that gave me the key. It was making the din common to all of them—the chittle-chottle of the water pump—and it amounted to a motorized palanquin. Mounted on the back was a compartment for passengers with a car door, windows all around, and padded upholstery within. It was painted a half dozen of the bright colors Hindus favor—pinks, yellows, blues.

I stared, I broke into laughter, I drew my conclusion. To make it new, to recognize no declared limit, to imagine and reimagine and then reimagine again: On the street in Veraval these began to suggest themselves as indelible traits, if there is any such thing. I thought of something a friend had recently told me. And I decided then how to name the tradition I have tried to describe.

"What has saved us all until now is the chance to choose eccentricity."

ECCENTRICITY IS EXPENSIVE, as any eccentric can tell you. Life exacts its costs, and they are frequently material. One way to describe the moment India has come to may be to say simply that it has tired, over the years, of paying the price of its preferences.

In Calcutta, I knew a tea grower named Sanjay Bansal who owned ten prosperous estates in Darjeeling. One by one he had shifted each from the old British method—overseas capital, bonded labor, mass production—back to the ancient tradition: self-sustaining farms and farmers, no chemicals, tea as a collaboration between man and nature. Among Sanjay's inspirations was the "spiritual agriculture" of Rudolf Steiner, the Austrian thinker, writer, and (fair to say) eccentric. "We're dismantling the Western model," Sanjay told me as we sipped this, that, and the other of his Darjeelings at a warehouse one day. "The people who will succeed in this country are the ones thinking differently."

So the eccentric tradition lives. Sanjay's tea is called Ambootia and sells in the best shops in Paris, London, and New York. But the tradition is not what we mean when we say "the new India." The new India wants more of the Western model, not less of it. In the new India one sometimes wishes the eccentric tradition could be photographed so as to look at it when it is gone. Gandhi, indeed, is known now mostly by way of iconic images—an effective way the world over of setting someone quietly aside. Yes, *jugaadi* are everywhere, but in the affection Indians have for them the first whiff of nostalgia is evident.

Urbanization and industrialization are "the two obsessions of a rising people." That is Emile Cioran, the Romanian writer, as he reflected on his own country in the 1930s. There is no suggestion that he had any thought for India or anywhere else in Asia. But he describes all Asians at the moment they have chosen to follow the West, from the Japanese of Meiji to the Indians since their reforms.

"Villagers don't want the village," a writer in Delhi named Dipankar Gupta, who is noted for his studies of the country-side, once told me. It is a blunt way to put what many say. Textile and silk weaving, carpet weaving, leatherwork, work with gems, brass work, ironwork, the making of brooms, pots, woven plates from the leaves of the local tree: There are many hundreds of crafts identified with village India, and it is said no one wants these, either. The power loom replaces the hand loom, and no one in the village knows how to operate the hand loom anymore—a wooden loom made by the father or grand-father of the last man to use it. Skills are lost; knowledge evap-orates. And this is not simply a matter of money, one hears over and over. It is status. The crafts are no longer ennobled, in a word—no longer invested with dignity. To aspire in an Indian village means to keep your son from learning the craft of your family or caste and hope he finds something else—a construc-tion job in Bombay, an IT job in one of the high-technology centers, a place in a BPO, meaning a business-processing office, an outsourcing operation.

Urban drift is hardly new in developing countries. But in India after the reforms it approached the proportions of a flood. There are slightly more than 600,000 villages in India, and not quite three-quarters of the nation's 1.1 billion people live in them. But roughly eight million Indians now move from village to city in a typical year—a new New York City per annum.

Indians have no habit of ripping down their old cities, as the Chinese do. The old cities bulge, each crumbly street a tourna-ment of horn blowers—incessant horns being the quintessen-tial sound of Indian aspiration. And next to the old cities come new ones, where the life of the new India gets lived. Hyderabad ranks with Bangalore as a center for information technology. But none of that is in Hyderabad proper: It is next door, in the new city known locally as Cyberabad. In Hyderabad you find the old city walls, the lively markets, the sixteenth-century mosque, a gleaming Hindu temple to compete with it. Cyberabad is made of tinted-glass boxes and not-quite-finished expressways. In between are communities that resemble California suburbs. By day, an office in Cyberabad; in the evening, a visit to the old city—dinner, perhaps, in the picturesque India one no longer lives in.

In Delhi, I once attended an urban-planning seminar at the invitation of a friend. The room was full of scholars, bureaucrats, bankers, lawyers, executives, experts in the life of cities. The talk was technocratic, but I found myself jotting down a few of the observations made.

"The need is to shift from poverty eradication to planning for prosperity," a professor of urban studies said.

"We don't really have an urban plan at all," a housing expert said, "but if we want to develop, we will urbanize."

A scholar from Harvard talked about "verticality." He said, "In Shanghai they are building upward. In New York we are building upward."

A banker said, "The idea that India will remain a rural environment is simply not realistic."

Then the housing expert again: "We have to start moving people faster and faster."

This is the new India thinking aloud. It is sequential India. It finds itself caught up in a process, and there is no talk of managing the process itself—only of how to cope within the process, as if the process were immutable. No one stops to think that human agency made the process and human agency can alter it. The process is Western, and it is inevitable: We are reminded, by way of its absence, that among the great gifts of the eccentric tradition has been the gift of imagination as it arises from the Indian ground like Sanjay Bansal's organic tea leaves.

Dipankar Gupta, the Delhi writer and scholar, once told me about a talk he gave to some NRIs—nonresident Indians, expatriates in New York. He spoke about the Indian middle class, which is commonly said to number 300 million. What does this mean, Gupta asked, when one is counted middle class with an income of eighty-seven American cents per day? What does "upper class" mean when two dollars and thirty cents daily makes one upper class? What does it mean that the IT industry, the beating heart of the new India, employs but three million people, or that all of 3 percent of households own cars?

Gupta was received badly among the NRIs. They objected to his numbers and questions. They flinched in the face of India as it is. He remembered as we spoke, a hot day in Delhi much later, how his audience sighed, asked no questions of their own, and left early with scarcely a murmur among them.

It is remarkable to discover the extent to which Indians—the technocrats and the executives and the urban elite—can fool themselves about the new India, "Incredible India." Stop worrying about poverty and prepare for prosperity? As Gandhi liked to put it, people with such thoughts do not know their India (which many Indians will admit, given there are so many Indias to know). The vision of a middle-class nation as India has come to have it is just this—a sort of vision. On any serious examination it is impossible that it will come to be, let alone be sustainable. Without bringing a lot of social science into it, the middle class in India probably numbers about 5 percent of the population—thirty million to fifty million people, a tenth or so of the official statistic. It would require the energy of another planet—one at the least—to bring the reality into line with the vision. Depending on which cities we count, India has grown nine or ten big ones in the six decades since independence. In the roundest of figuring, is it to grow eighty or ninety or a hundred more to "urbanize" in the next half century? Migration to the cities has come to about 200 million since independence. This, too, is unsustainable. In the middle of our century a half-billion Indians are still likely to dwell in the villages that are supposed to disappear.

"We want to bask in the glory of being a modern society," Gupta reflected that afternoon, "without taking the trouble of making ourselves modern." This is the new India in a phrase. So we must take "Incredible India" precisely as it claims to be— beyond believing.

Many Indians, as Sanjay Bansal would say, are thinking differently about these matters. They are another part of the new India—less advertised, less enraptured by their own song, but present and accounted for nonetheless. They are what has become of the eccentric tradition.

"Look closely and we are sitting on a time bomb. We have twenty years, twenty-five at most, to avert a crisis."

This observation belongs to a man named Satyan Mishra. He was young, energetic, committed to his different thinking. I grew to know Satyan over many years, sometimes talking long hours in his Delhi office or in his apartment, sometimes traveling together through the countryside to this or that of his projects. Satyan is committed to the Indian village. He is partly a Gandhian and partly a twenty-first-century techie, perfectly at home with modern things. I never asked him if he would mind being called an eccentric, but he was one in the way we are using the term.

Satyan's view was simple and sophisticated all at once. He would not put it this way, but his work in the villages reflects a belief that Cioran's old thought about cities and industries and rising aspirations cannot hold for India. The way of the West cannot be imported as Japan and China did so. India must be original once more, eccentric once more, for it must find its future somewhere in its past—an eccentric endeavor, truly.

THE SADDEST VILLAGE I have ever seen, though not the poorest by a long way, is called Sandur. It lies a day's train journey north of Bangalore. I remember telling a Bangalore friend named Saritha Rai that I was making the trip.

"To see the mining," Saritha replied.

"The textiles."

"Right," she said. "I knew it was one or the other."

That is Sandur. It was long known for the bright clothing made by the Lambani, tribal people who migrated south from Rajasthan and Gujarat many centuries ago. Most of us have seen Lambani pieces. They are full of pattern and color, and there are mirrors and bangles stitched into some of the designs. The craft comes down from mother to daughter (never the sons), and it is more than clothing: It is the way Lambani women know who they are and tell others who they are.

"Gandhi came here once," a local man named Shiva Prakash told me when I arrived. "Afterward he said, 'See Sandur in September.' That would have been after the monsoon. Everything would've been green." Gandhi might have gone for the textiles. The mahatma loved khadi, hand-spun and handwoven cotton, and khadi is made locally, too. But not many people go to Sandur for the textiles anymore, and there is no point going for the greenery because there is scarcely any left.

For many miles around Sandur, everything is covered with the rust-colored dust of oxidized iron ore. Roads are packed with it, windows are fogged with it, the leaves of trees are coated with it. Mining has overrun Sandur. In the center of the village one can detect only the bones of the kind of place Gandhi must have seen. When it rains now in Sandur, the puddles are ponds of rust. Gandhi and his remark are points of pride among the residents of Sandur, everyone quoting the mahatma a little differently. But it is pride in what once was, not in what is—not in what Sandur has done to itself or had done to it. However Gandhi had put it, what he said could not be said now.

The textile place I wanted to visit was a cooperative. There was a dimly lit shop, an office, a warehouse, and a small factory. Lambani women sat at tables and stitched blouses, bags, skirts, and hats to the specifications that companies from Delhi and elsewhere had ordered. It was a little like Fabindia and its contracts with village weavers. One finds variations on the theme all over India.

I fell into a conversation with some Lambani women. I wondered aloud whether it was so important to preserve the old craft.

"Preserve the craft," one named Shanti Bai said, considering the thought. "It's practically dead now. It's a way to make a living."

I wanted to know about the designs sent from the cities. It is a curious point of contention among those trying to find a new way for the old village crafts: If you dictate the designs to suit a shop in Delhi or New York, are the craftspeople not reduced to so many pairs of hands, deprived of their brains and imaginations?

"The Westerners change the colors," Shanti replied. "They want muted blues and different products. But it's the same skill. We're happy enough."

Confidence amid change and loss, but also fatefulness: Things had changed and been lost before, they must have been, and our change is simply more of it, the "no change amid change."

In the office I met the man who looked after the cooperative. He introduced himself as Veeranna. It turned out that Veeranna worked for the company that was mining the iron ore around Sandur, and the company had set up the cooperative. That was in the mid-1980s. In the shop there was a plastic banner with a picture of Gandhiji in his simple, slightly bent spectacles.

"They've gained from the area," Veeranna said a bit laconically. "They want to put some back to society."

We talked of many things: the designs from outside, where the women came from—they lived in hamlets called *thanda*—and day rates as against pay for piecework. I wanted to ask Veeranna something I was not sure I could convey. It had to do with the fate of culture and tradition when these become a self-conscious undertaking. A friend in Calcutta had given me a word for it: He called it "museumization."

I started toward my point but did not have to finish.

Veeranna said, "We're making museum pieces, if that's what you mean. What we're doing for the crafts is like a drop in the ocean. They're pieces for people with money and a taste for traditional things."

It was late afternoon when I left the cooperative, and the road was dense with trucks—huge things, with tires the height of a teenage boy. I asked Shiva about it, for I had seen no trucks when I arrived. There were ten trucks to every passenger car, Shiva reckoned. It had become impossible to use the roads, and they had passed a law: The mines could operate during the day, but the trucks could begin only at four o'clock and then drive all night until dawn. Demand for ore in China and in India itself had changed everything. There were fifty thousand people in the villages scattered around Sandur; thirty thousand were migrant workers. And almost everyone, migrant or not, now depended on the mining.

Night fell as we drove to the town where I had a hotel. The trucks had turned the roads into obstacle courses of deep craters, and we went slowly. In the villages the migrants stood in groups: bare feet, sarongs, no shirts, soft drinks and slices of fruit in their hands. These were the miners, done for the day. In the darkness between villages I watched the horizon. Along it an orange glow reached skyward, as if a city lay at the end of the vast, empty countryside. These were blast furnaces. Steel was the new industry around Sandur, following the ore. It reminded me, suddenly, of the Yahata works in Kitakyushu and the spell the light and sparks cast over the Japanese for so many years.

Later I visited some of the *thanda*, the Lambani settlements. None was far from the main road. Turn down a stony lane and you entered another time: an earthen house and then rubble, another house, then more rubble; no electricity, a community spigot, poultry and goats wandering the paths and into the houses. In a *thanda* called Kadirampur, I met a group of women like those at the factory in Sandur. But they did not have a cooperative, or a piecework rate, or designs coming from Delhi. If they sold anything, it was by way of street vendors catering to the tourists coming to Hampi, the nearby ruins of a fourteenth-century empire.

A woman named Mangi Bai turned out to be talkative. Mangi was sixty, she thought, possibly seventy. We had the same sort of conversation I had had at the cooperative, but it came out very differently.

"I prefer the older dresses," Mangi said. "Old food style, old living style, old customs, old dress style. Modern dress comes from factories. It harms our way of life. Old things we can make, modern things we can't."

"What about your children, then?"

A woman named Yamuni Bai responded. She was fifty, with a handsome face. She seemed more agreeable than Mangi, who had a crusty manner.

"I've got one daughter and two sons," Yamuni said. "My girl I want to do the same thing. My boys I want to be doctors and businessmen."

Mangi was not quite satisfied with this. She found something surrendering in Yamuni, I sensed.

Mangi said, "Nothing's wrong with modern dress. Those who like it let them wear it. But I don't like to wear the saree, and I don't like to promote them."

Mangi paused and looked around the group. Then: "We're

marginals. We like to be in groups—to work in groups, to stay in groups. We believe in groups."

Then Mangi looked straight at me. "I don't like the modern world," she said.

Then Mangi Bai smiled.

I HAVE CALLED SANDUR SAD. I mean this the way Shiv Visvanathan used the word. "The moment of celebration is a moment of sadness," he had said.

For a long time after I went to Sandur, I reflected on the story Veeranna had told me at the cooperative. It is easy enough to say the old crafts were on life support—an ornament, a charity, a small dependency. But it is not so simple. The spirit resides in things, as Gandhi taught. The one is not over here and the other over there. The new industry with its trucks and grit and mess and ruination: It went on symbiotically with the old crafts. It was by keeping alive the latter that the company and the people who worked for it coped, to the extent they could, with the modern. "We have our own things amid all these modern things," they could say.

Women understand this symbiosis, it seemed to me. The Lambani women seemed, indeed, perfectly clear on the matter. Women are the vessels of tradition in India. The past is inscribed on them; their bodies are sites of cultural preservation and social pride. Only a woman nowadays could say, "I don't like the modern world." It is the woman's place to articulate such a thing—to say what cannot be said. It is as important to the miners that their wives wear the old dresses as it is to the wives themselves.

There is another way to put these thoughts. The village of Sandur had entered sequential time. The trucks and smelters and furnaces had "sequentialized" it, so it had a past given one value and a present and future given another. With sequence had come the madness, and with the madness the sadness.

· · ·

WHEN I FIRST MET Satyan Mishra, it was to go to a village called Kalan Wali. He was twenty-nine then, and he had started something called Drishtee, which means "vision" in Hindi. Drishtee was a case of Indian ambiguity: It was a company but also a foundation; it was a company and a foundation but also an NGO, a nongovernmental organization; it was all of these but also a government contractor. Drishtee was Satyan's way into India's villages.

Kalan Wali was up in Haryana state, six hours on bumpy roads north of Delhi. Kalan Wali's farmers did well for themselves. The fields were irrigated and neatly kept—a bright, deep green the season I was there. The village square was crowded with camels and muddy tractors. There was an open market for produce; grain and raw cotton were piled high on the pavement.

Near the square I met a woman named Alka Narang. She was twenty-five, and she sat in a ten-foot-square room with a concrete floor and a window giving onto a dusty side street. There was a table with a computer, a modem, a printer, and a telephone on it. There were plastic chairs and, on the wall above the table, a map of Haryana: These were the things of Alka's livelihood.

Ten or fifteen times a day, six days a week, villagers would arrive to request a service from Sirsa, the district office, which was twenty-five miles away. If they were BPLs—Indians below the poverty line—they would qualify for a loan to buy a buffalo, and they might apply. They might need an identity card, or a driver's license, or a land record, or a loan—common request, this—to acquire sheep. Maybe they needed to file a complaint: The irrigation system had collapsed; the local teacher was not showing up. Alka's job and Drishtee's project were to send these requests to Sirsa. And this was something very new in Kalan Wali.

In the old days it had been difficult for the four thousand people of Kalan Wali to use government services. The bus to Sirsa cost thirty rupees—not quite sixty cents—and one lost a day's work. In Sirsa there might be a bribe to pay. And a villager never knew how long he or she would have to follow a bureaucrat around or whether the bureaucrat would be there. Most villagers in Kalan Wali, as elsewhere, never bothered.

Alka and Satyan had changed that. Drishtee's services cost ten rupees (administrative complaint) to twenty-five (driver's license). These were sums Satyan fixed to sustain the project but keep the price below the effective cost of government services before Drishtee came along. So there was no more bus ride, no lost time in the fields, no more bribing when one got to Sirsa. Over time, the idea took. "Slowly but surely," Alka told me as we talked, "I've come to be accepted."

To use modern technology to bring the political process to remote villages—this was something I had never seen. It seemed another example of *jugaad*. There was also Satyan's "business model." India at this time—early in our century—had made itself a laboratory for finding imaginative ways for the public and private sectors to collaborate. Again, it was a matter of creative, purposeful ambiguity. And Satyan, with his contract with Haryana state, had shown me one of these ways.

But there was something in Kalan Wali I could not quite register. I concluded it was the politics of the thing.

"Satyan," I said, "you can call this the rural extension of democracy, but you can't make people pay for ordinary rights You can't turn the political process into a commodity, or democracy into an item in a market."

I remember how evenly Satyan replied. We were in a car, on the way to another village.

"You have to start where you are. We identified a need and then determined how to fulfill it."

Over some years I saw many other Drishtee projects. The "model" was modified, always: From connecting villages to the district office it went to computer-training classes in village shopfronts and then on to mobile telephone services. In one village I watched high-school students read their examination results on the Internet. The street outside was a mix of motorcycles, cows, cow dung, and carts on bicycle wheels selling ices. At the end of the street was the pond where the cows had drunk and the children had swum for centuries. Always on these journeys the thought was the same: Bring the village along rather than leave it behind; use what technology is to hand.

I eventually understood what had left me faintly flummoxed after my visit to Kalan Wali. The thought came after visits to many villages, but especially one called Saurath. If Sandur lived in sequential time, Satyan had introduced me to heterogeneous time as it might survive in India. He was the first to immerse me in it.

SAURATH IS A day's journey from Patna, one of the cities (along with Allahabad, Benares, and others) that lie on the heavily traveled route between Delhi and Calcutta. We set out at dawn toward the Himalayas and the border with Nepal. By the afternoon we had left the Ganges plain and begun to climb. Saurath is high—in the green foothills on the southern slopes of the great range.

Satyan spent a long time telling me about Saurath before sending me off with a Jeep and a driver. This was different from the other projects—more, much more, than "e-governance" and assorted electronic services. Saurath was his mother's village, for one thing. Satyan knew it with a special affection. And it was Saurath he had chosen as the place he could show India that its villages could go on living.

One evening Satyan told me the long story of how the Indian village had come unglued. It began when the British altered land arrangements in the eighteenth century. In essence—it is a complex history—those who worked the land were alienated from it. This produced a class of landlords—wealthy, upper caste—called *zamindars*. The *zamindars* lived well, dressed in the British fashion, and grew fond of imported goods. After independence they became manufacturers in the cities, and the waves of migration began. The villages were marginalized. Nobody could any longer buy the things other villagers made, so less got made. Self-sustaining communities turned into collections of tiny plots—divided and subdivided and subdivided again. A certain ecology that had endured for two millennia was destroyed in a matter of two centuries.

There are many villages in India where one cannot imagine anything had ever thrived. Saurath is not one of these. Eighty percent of its young people have left, yet a certain coherence to village life remains undisturbed. Down its sandy, shaded pathways, in its ponds and brick walls and thatched-roof houses, the village as it was lingers, the village as it must have been.

The Brahman castes favored Saurath in centuries past. It was cool, green, a bit bucolic. In the fifteenth century a maharaja built a *sabha*, as they call it locally—an agora, a town square—where the privileged castes for many miles around used to gather. The *sabha*, elsewhere called a *chotro*, remains. Next to it is a lake with a little ghat leading down to it. Both the lake and the ghat were also built by the maharaja.

Saurath is still noted for its *sabha*. And in a certain way it was the *sabha*, the spirit of it without the caste connection, that Satyan wanted to bring back to life. His "model," this time, was very technocratic and very twenty-first century. The people of Saurath were to invest in a community company, each share worth 10,000 rupees—about $220. The investments were to go toward what we now call public goods—electricity, water, health care, irrigation ditches. They were to be an incentive for people to "stay back"—remain in the village—and from their number would come a group of "micro-entrepreneurs." Small markets would form—for locally made goods, locally grown goods, locally caught fish, locally generated services, goods and services brought in wholesale from the outside. The village would regain its ecology.

Satyan said, "We should have enough reason to stay back, and then we will have a market to serve the people staying back."

Drishtee had already begun some parts of the Saurath project when I went to see it. There was a doctor in the village and another who visited, a small power plant that burned bamboo, an irrigation well, a plan to build a school. The most interesting thing by a long way was the BPO—the business-processing office. This proved another plunge into heterogeneous time.

It was in a house that must have been built not long after the Raj, a whitewashed place in the Anglo–Indian style. You walked down a crunchy drive and across a covered veranda. In a room at the rear were two banks of computers and telephones, ten of each in each row. Outside was the bamboo-burning generator, rattling away, and beyond that a farmer and his oxen milling pulse, a seed Indians use to season rice.

There were a half-dozen BPOs—those working in outsourcing offices are called this, too—and we got into a conversation. They were all in their mid-thirties, five men and a woman, and they answered calls for companies far away, they did surveys, they did data entry, they edited texts and letters, there was some quality-control work.

A man named Dilip had been a supervisor at a production line in Delhi and had come home. Asha was a housewife taken with the idea of a globally connected village. Passupati loved farmers and had returned after some years in Patna. He consulted by telephone with farmers around Saurath—about seeds and fertilizers and irrigation, about planting and harvesting and the weather. They were bright, these people. They could have made their way in Bangalore or Bombay easily enough.

"Doesn't everyone want to move to the cities?"

At this, they all chimed in.

Dilip said, "I make less here, but I live better. I belong here. Life in the city: There's too much stress to it."

Passupati said, "There's not enough opportunity here; otherwise people wouldn't go. Ninety percent of villagers would rather stay back."

And Asha: "All the facilities in the town—if we could get them here, it would be much better. And the pollution in the town—of course there's that."

IT WAS TO BE some time before Saurath could be counted a success or a failure, and Satyan was counting in years.

Before I set out from Patna, he had said by telephone, "Ask them what they think. Tell me if they're truly interested. I ask, but I never know if I'm getting the truth."

I asked. I did my espionage. And I reported back that the Saurath villagers seemed interested but that it was all somewhat of an abstraction. A community company? Shares at ten thousand rupees apiece? Projects someone from the outside dreams up? The moment of enlightenment had not yet arrived.

Satyan seemed disappointed but not surprised. In the posing of the question, I reflected, lay his doubt, and so his answer.

I turned Saurath this way and that for a long time after my visit, joining those many who wonder about the fate of India's villages. In the best of outcomes, the best villages will become small towns, and the best small towns will become small cities—another way to "urbanize" India. But maybe the fate of the village should be left to the village. Maybe a project such as Saurath was simply a matter of "museumization." Maybe Saurath would turn out to be an Edsel of a thing—eccentric enough but done in by its own eccentricity.

I did not know and do not. I do not think India or anyone in it knows. Saurath is a dream or a sensible idea. No one wants to be in the village; everyone wants to be in the village. People should stay in the village; people should have a choice; people should go . . .

In Delhi, Dipankar Gupta had spoken once of *telos*, the Greek for purpose, the intent or end of something. There is *telos* and there is *techne*, the method of making a thing. *Telos* always lies in front, unattained, a principle requiring that we continue our striving.

"Modernity is not a finished product," Gupta had mused that afternoon. "The *telos* of modernity is what I'm talking about. We can't see it as 'done.' It's a constantly moving target."

This is India's gift to us, offered from East to West and from East to East. It is in the space made by a moving, never-fixed thing that India goes on toward its modernity. It is by way of this space that it has been trapped by neither modern things nor old notions of the spirit—not yet, in any case, not entirely.

Readings

Bharucha, Rustom. *Another Asia*. New Delhi, 2006.
Chatterjee, Partha. "Our Modernity." Rotterdam and Dakar, 1997.
———. *The Politics of the Governed*. New Delhi, 2004.
Ci Jiwei. *Dialectic of the Chinese Revolution*. Stanford, CA, 1994.
Fabian, Johannes. *Time and the Other*. New York, 1983.
Gadamer, Hans-Georg. *Truth and Method*. New York, 1992.
Lange, Frederick Albert. *The History of Materialism*. London, 1925.
Levenson, Joseph R. *Confucian China and Its Modern Fate*. London, 1958; Berkeley, CA, 1964, 1965.
Nandy, Ashis. *The Intimate Enemy*. New Delhi, 1983.
———. *Time Warps*. New Brunswick, NJ, 2002.
Nishitani Keiji. *Religion and Nothingness*. Berkeley, CA, 1982.
———. *The Self-overcoming of Nihilism*. Albany, NY, 1990.
Sen, Amartya. *Development as Freedom*. New York, 1999.
Wagner, Roy. *The Invention of Culture*. Englewood Cliffs, NJ, 1975.

The Buddhas at Qixia

And we carry all our past behind us, as that which we are
no longer. If we make a theme of this past, it becomes
imaginary.

—SARTRE, *War Diaries* (1940)

1

IN THE WESTERN HILLS, those semisacred mounds outside
Beijing that look as if they await one of the old scholar-
painters, ancient processional roads lead from temple to temple. The emperors kept them up over many centuries. One
climbs a hill called Ma'an Shan, Saddle Hill, atop which sits a
much-noted Buddhist monastery.

Jietai Si dates to the seventh century. The monks loved the
pines around the monastery so much they gave them names.
Just below Jietai Si is something scarcely known but just as
interesting. It is a stone gate arched over the processional road.
It stands about thirty feet high, and beneath its Ming eaves it is
carved with dragons, lotuses, and rows of figures. Bits of color
remain. It seems to have marked the place where a traveler
would enter or leave the sacred space of the monastery. On
the outside the figures depict people of various stations and
professions—profane humanity—while on the inside these are
all transformed into Buddhas.

An inscription dates the gate to the twenty-seventh year of
the reign of the emperor Wanli, which puts it at 1599. This was
among the last of Wanli's attentive years. He later dissipated
and grew so obese he was unable to stand. Then the Manchu
came knocking at the northern doors of Wanli's domain. It was
the beginning of the end for the Ming, the beginning of the
beginning for the Qing.

When I was first taken to Wanli's gate, we could not find the
track leading to it. The place had been neglected for a half

century or more—ignored by the villagers living nearby, over-
looked by all but the most diligent visitors. The processional
road—splendid slabs of stone worn smooth—was strewn with
rubble. During the Cultural Revolution the gate had been
defaced in the most literal manner: Red Guards had chiseled
off the features of the figures carved into the columns, as high
as they could reach without a ladder.

There are places like Wanli's gate all over China. In the
mountains north of Nanjing there is a temple called Qixia,
which dates to the fifth century. Behind it, across an immense
rock face, are grottoes and caves carved with hundreds of Buddhas. And again: heads hacked off, limbs snapped, faces obliter-
ated. I saw Qixia on an autumn afternoon with an artist named
Zhuang Hongxing. Zhuang had been purged during the Cultural Revolution, all his work destroyed. Years later, when he
could paint again, he had gone to Qixia and done watercolors
of the grottoes.

We walked the place together. Many of the Buddhas were
still disfigured, but some restoration had begun. The work was
crude: Arms and heads made of twenty-first-century plaster
were attached to ancient torsos of stone—some of it a soiled
but luminous white, some the palest ocher, remains of the old
paint.

Zhuang went close, passing slowly from statue to statue,
staring as if the Buddhas were long-lost friends. I could not
tell which made him sadder: the Red Guards' ravages or the
restorations.

He felt some of the pieces with his fingers and began to call
back to me: "This is original . . . This wasn't here twenty years
ago . . . These are replaced . . . This is real . . . This one's a fake:
There's a steel rod inside it."

QIXIA, WANLI'S GATE, and places like them have captivated me
for many years. I visit Ma'an Shan whenever I am in Beijing
and time allows, for some new perspective on China and its lay-

ered past seems always to emanate from the faceless figures near the ground and those higher up with blurred features—weather having done over centuries what Red Guards did one mindless afternoon.

Centuries of use, then disuse and neglect, a sudden deface-ment, then more neglect. The latest layer came in the middle of this past decade. A preservation agency in Beijing declared the processional road a cultural relic. Six months later a stone was set near the gate with a plaque fixed to it. Then came the restoration crews. When I last saw the gate, it was braced with steel supports, and the faces of the faceless figures were being redone. As at Qixia, the erasure was being erased.

We ordinarily think of the mutilation of artifacts and the manipulation of the past as the aberrations of Maoist zealots, obsessed as they were with "the four olds." The mess they left is evident, but we miss the point if we leave it there. Qixia and the stone gate have something more to tell us—something perti-nent not only to the Cultural Revolution, or indeed to China and the Chinese, but to much of Asia. What does it mean that people would try to destroy all traces of their past and lose all relation to it? Where does such an impulse originate? One can ask this among the Buddhas at Qixia, but one can ask it just as plausibly in the middle of most Chinese cities today or in most Japanese cities and towns, wartime destruction notwithstand-ing. The context is different, but one can ask it in India, too.

The starkest case of a compulsively destroyed past in all of history is almost certainly the book burning ordered by Qin Shihuang in 213 B.C. Qin unified China by bringing six warring states under his control. He assembled the Great Wall in the north and developed a system of canals in the south. He im-posed a uniform script. When he built roads, the ruts had to be the same width everywhere. Then he destroyed all contending schools of thought. The administrative records of the other states were burned. So were all philosophical and historical texts other than those Qin Shihuang sanctioned. Hundreds of

scholars were buried alive. "How regrettable!" a contemporary
account lamented. "Only the records of Qin remain, and
these do not record the days and months, and are brief and
incomplete."

China takes its name from Qin's dynasty. With erasing and
regret did it first become one.

Qin Shihuang's point seems to have been the elimination of
"otherness." He wanted to expunge heterodoxy from history.
He destroyed the past to save the past—the Qin past. And he
did this to destroy the prospect of any kind of alternative way
forward. Qin Shihuang understood: If you do not have a past,
you do not have a future.

The impulse to destroy the past even as one asserts its worth
has been a prevalent part of Asia's modern experience. But it
is different from what we find in the story of China's first
emperor. Qin Shihuang, safe to conclude, thought a lot of the
Qin way of doing things. Since the West arrived in the East in
the nineteenth century, it has been more complex. In the modern period one might ennoble one's past even while destroying
or burying it. And to obliterate one's own history, one's path
into the present, has been at some level an expression of self-
contempt, of resignation. There is some other measure of self-
worth against which one fails. The defacing of Qixia's Buddhas,
understood in its largest meaning, reveals a deeply felt sense of
inferiority, a trauma that came in the course of an encounter
with an "other" who was seen—in past and present both—as
superior.

We must return briefly to the matter of chronology. What
happened when the West brought progress—sequential time,
Enlightenment time—eastward? And what were the consequences of what happened?

The first of these questions is quickly answered. With the
coming of "progress," Asian thinking turned upside down, like
an hourglass. People shifted from past-consciousness to future-
consciousness. If we bring the thought of utopia into it, utopia

was to be found no longer in what had been but in what was to come. The change was a nineteenth-century change, but some dates are oddly specific as a shorthand to understanding. Japan went decisively from past-consciousness to future-consciousness on the morning of August 15, 1945. Before the surrender, all was spirit and the hallowed ancestors; afterward, it was a matter of making the "miracle." In China the date is October 1, 1949. When Mao took Beijing, he institutionalized future-consciousness: Heaven lies ahead of us, comrades; the state that has burdened you since Qin Shihuang will wither away.

The consequences of this shift from past thinking to future thinking came to three. It would be difficult to overstate their importance.

The past was destabilized when the future became the main event. It had once been conveyed through the meticulous records of able administrators as to how things had always been done. With the turning forward, the past became narrative, a story. And there was no fixedness to it. The state became the bearer of the story, just as it had always kept the records, and a dysfunctional tie between the past and power took hold. The past could be destroyed or invented, edited, augmented, airbrushed in or out, changed and changed again. Asians did not invent the inventing of history (unless Qin Shihuang gets the credit). But the practice has had an especially profound effect on them.

The self was destabilized, too. Modernity required one to pass from a state of "always was"—fate, place—to a state of becoming. As aspiring Asians thought of it, an old self had to be put in a camphor chest for special occasions, and a new self had to be "put on." The early-modern literature in Japan and China is filled with characters who are "finding their way" in this fashion. It was not until after the war, when the Japanese wondered among themselves why they had so blindly followed the emperor, that they began to talk of *shutai-sei*—selfhood, the autonomous, judging, deciding self, selves that could have said no.

Questions of self had to do with questions of belonging. This, finally, was also disrupted. One had belonged differently during the many centuries of past-consciousness. A household, a clan, a village, a craft, an enterprise, later a company or a factory unit—this was belonging. Scholars call this an assurance society, one based on fixed ties with familiars. We can call it simply "the old belonging." Japan had been a gathering of households—and so a household itself—until the second half of the nineteenth century. India was an idea (for a long time someone else's), and in China the old saying held: "Heaven is high and the emperor is far away." Belonging was local.

The coming of the modern changed this. One belonged, suddenly, to a nation. A nation is a "trust society," as the scholars say, one based not on familiarity but on reliable behavior among strangers. For simplicity's sake we can call this "the new belonging." Even now one detects the tension that arose a century and more ago between the old and the new belonging. The nation-state, truly, was the oddest and most unwieldy of all the things Asians imported from the West in the nineteenth and early twentieth centuries. And among its least comfortable features was that one was supposed to belong differently. The past would be less than useless: It would give a bad appearance and hold one back. It was *tu*, like an embarrassing uncle in from the village. The village was old, the nation new. This was how, at least, the matter was thought of.

IN THE SPRING OF 1882, just as the Third Republic was turning France into modern France roughly as we know it, Ernest Renan delivered a lecture at the Sorbonne that, at thirty pages, remains among his most noted works. Renan, by then renowned as a thinker and historian, titled his discourse "Qu'est-ce qu'une nation?"—"What Is a Nation?" His answer has proven its provocative worth many times in the decades since he offered it.

Renan addressed numerous concerns when he spoke that day in March long ago. He talked of "the error most grave in confounding race and nation." He talked about the irrelevance of a common language, or religion, or commercial interest, or natural geographic frontiers in recognizing what a nation was. A nation, properly understood, amounted to "a moral consciousness," Renan argued—"a spiritual principle." This made him a believer in nations and nationality but emphatically not a nationalist. A nation, he said in a famous metaphor, was "a daily plebiscite"—a profession of belief and belonging each citizen makes by participating in everyday life.

The best-known parts of Renan's talk had to do with remembering and forgetting. And it was the latter, perhaps surprisingly, that Renan chose to emphasize. "Forgetting, and I would say even historical lapses, are essential in the creation of a nation," he asserted, "and it is thus that the pursuit of historical studies is often a danger." The most quoted passage in "What Is a Nation?" comes in what must have been another minute or two during Renan's time at the lectern: "So the essence of a nation is that all of its individuals have many things in common, and also that they forget certain things."

Renan had it exactly right for a man at the center of his time. Nations were inventing themselves at that moment. France was going to be France because it remembered the Revolution but would forget some of what had happened before it. America in 1882 had just saved itself, and it would remain one by settling—wrongly, we can now see—on what had to be forgotten. But Renan died eight years before the twentieth century began. And we know now—now, as the era of nation-states begins to look as if it has a beginning, a middle, and an end—the high cost of forgetting. Renan remains right about forgetting, but we must now say "dreadfully right."

The past century in Asia is heavily scarred with erasures. Almost everywhere, history is a smudge. The Chinese remember some things resolutely and other things, even very recent events, scarcely at all. Japan made itself the world's most knotted-up nation, fair to say, because it could not decide how to remember the twentieth century. Remembering and forgetting in India are so densely layered now that the conversation is less about history than about the history of many different histories. Which history do we claim as our own and which do we forget? Which past is truly our past? How these are answered determines not much short of everything for Indians (and many others) in the twenty-first century.

Not quite a century ago, in a book aptly titled *America's Coming-of-Age*, the critic Van Wyck Brooks began a lifelong search for what he would soon name "a usable past," whether discovered or invented. This is Asia's predicament today— predicament because it must decide what a past that it can use to see the future would be, what would constitute it, what it would have to include.

In Xi'an once, I watched one afternoon as visitors to Qin Shihuang's ancient capital strolled the grounds that surround a seventh-century pagoda known as Great Wild Goose. Here and there were statues depicting characters and scenes from the old China, the undisrupted China of centuries earlier. There were musicians with traditional instruments, village wrestlers, a husband and wife at home in their hut. Chinese tourists stared and laughed, took each other's pictures, or (the nimbler among them) climbed around these tableaux in bronze.

It was the strangest of sights. What could it be like to look upon a theme-park version of one's past and laugh the slightly disturbed laugh of one greeting a faintly familiar stranger? I thought, not so oddly, of Yasukuni Shrine in Tokyo, the memorial to Japan's war dead: a bucolic rendition of the past with the din and towers of an immense, reinvented city all around it.

There is little mistaking the search Asians have embarked

upon for an authentic past amid the wreckage and erasures and self-denials of the modern era. The running theme is origins. "Who are we, when we take off all we have 'put on'?" This is the question Asians ask. A friend in Tokyo, a longtime correspondent for an American newspaper, quit and withdrew quietly from the capital to study for the Shinto priesthood. One finds Confucian revivalists all over China—dressing in the old robes, bowing the old bows to elders.

Without diminishing the importance of tradition, we must dismiss most of this as of little use. Xi'an is history Disneyfied. Yasukuni, as a rendering of the past if not as a memorial, is another theme park. Neither does erasing the erasures of earlier times bring much benefit: It simply adds another layer of forgetting.

What is Asia's usable past, then? Where to find it?

If Asians are truly to know themselves—which is to say, to come of age—they will have to come to terms with their miscegenation. The past is made of every moment up to the one we live in, the moment we know as "now." Each speck of our past is part of what makes us who we are. Wanli's gate counts. Its defilement counts, as does the self-hatred the defilement reflects. And now the restoration counts, and the plaque set in the rock nearby. It all comes to the gate as it is, China as it is, and Asia as it is. We honor tradition only when we add to it. The rest is mere convention, unalive.

2

IN 1885, THREE YEARS AFTER Renan spoke at the Sorbonne, Japan was beginning to look unlike Japan—or a lot like another, new Japan.

Apart from all the building and striving in everyday life, it was acquiring the apparatus of a modern nation. Within a few years it would have a constitution: it liked Germany's, having inspected many. It would have a peerage—counts, barons, and so forth, again taken from the Germans. The constitution would provide for a Diet, a legislature, and there would be limited suffrage. Within a decade Japan would begin amassing an empire. Nations had colonies—1885 being an acquisitive year for Europeans—and Japan would have its colonies.

Fukuzawa Yukichi, who had already coined his term *bunmei*, civilization, wrote a newspaper item that same year called "Datsu-A ron." It translates variously. It comes into English as "Good-Bye Asia" or "Leaving Asia." The translation of Fukuzawa's piece favored by Japanese scholars is titled "On Departure from Asia."

"The wind of Western civilization has gradually proceeded eastward," Fukuzawa began. "Nowhere is there a blade of grass or a tree not blown by this wind."

A little further on, this: "Civilization is like an epidemic of measles . . . Even if we try to ward off its evil effects at this stage, what means have we? None whatever."

The problem came down to the old conventions—Confucianism and past-consciousness. None of that matched well with modern "civilization." Japan had tossed the old ways aside "and adopted a new mode of existence in Asia." This was *datsu-A*. It meant, specifically, leaving China and Korea behind. "The people of these two countries do not know how to reform themselves," Fukuzawa wrote. "They have no possible way to preserve their independence."

And so Fukuzawa proceeded to his fateful conclusion:

> In the eyes of civilized Westerners, because these three countries are adjacent to each other, they are sometimes all the same . . . Our immediate policy, therefore, should be to lose no time in waiting for the enlightenment of our neighboring countries to join them in developing Asia, but rather to depart from their ranks and cast our lot with the civilized countries of the West . . .

We should deal with them exactly as the Westerners do. Those with bad companions cannot avoid bad reputation. We must repudiate the bad companions of East Asia.

One may, to put the kindest face on it, liken *datsu-A* to the old English conundrum: another island nation wondering whether it was with the mainland or not. But *datsu-A* was a more complex proposition. Fukuzawa delivered a weighty indictment of a great many people from whom Japan had learned and absorbed much over many centuries. It would be difficult indeed to illustrate more plainly how the arrival of the West alienated Asians from their past and themselves. The great borrowing from the mainland—from China and from China via Korea—had gone on for about fourteen centuries at the time Fukuzawa wrote. Suddenly Japan was not part of Asia.

NEITHER WAS JAPAN to be Japan as it had been. Many things would have to change if it were going to leave Asia. Things would be left behind and things added, for this was a time of many invented traditions. A constitutional monarchy would require a proper monarch, so the emperor would move from ancient obscurity in Kyoto to reside in the shogun's palace in Tokyo: the Meiji Restoration, thus. New rites, if this is not an oxymoron, were established. There was a new calendar, which would turn the year back to 1 at the start of each imperial reign. Japan still lives in two kinds of time, two chronologies: the sequential time it took up from the West and the circular time it invented to plant the emperor firmly in the consciousness of his subjects.

One of the truly attractive things about native Japanese tradition—the tradition that predates even the great borrowing from China—was its apparent ease in matters to do with sex and gender. This is very likely to extend back to the foundational myths, which centered on a sun goddess. There is much evidence of matriarchal power in early, pre-Sinified Japan. Men and women were at home with each other. Love and intimacy were accessible in the most touchingly innocent way. The early poetry attests to this over and over. But this, too, had to go if the new Japan was to be a nation the way Westerners made nations. It would not do, this feminine thread of ease and delight. The Meiji Restoration was led by samurai, who drew their traditions from the warrior class in Tang dynasty China. Samurai tradition became the root of modern Japanese tradition, then. The older tradition was erased. This is why, strange but fair to say, modern Japan has made itself so singularly wanting in intimacy. On the way to making a nation, the Japanese forgot the way they had once known so well how to love.

The most fundamental forgetting Japan has done in the modern era has to do with its understanding of nature. This is a complex topic, because Asia's traditional conception of nature is so at variance with the West's and because humanity's relationship with the physical world is so basic to the way we think. A Japanese scholar put the point with admirable simplicity in view of its complications. Modern Japan, he said, was "baptized by science."

In the Western mind, nature is considered an object. It is outside of us, and so it is alien to us and we to it. Man is nature's master—a thought found in the Old Testament—and so he must act upon it. We call our means of asserting ourselves upon the material world "science." As Nietzsche put it many times, science is the humanization of nature. And there is nothing, we believe, that science cannot do and nowhere it should not go.

Asia's traditional idea of humanity and nature was very different: nature was all, humanity a part of it. There was no alienation, no subject-object relationship. One did not act upon nature so much as proceed according to its flow. Nature was, in Nietzsche's terminology, dehumanized. Certain values arose from this thought, paradoxes for non-Easterners: "the practice of inaction," "the doing of doing nothing." There is much Buddhism to be detected in this, and in Japan's case some Zen. If one wants truly to observe a flower or a tree, one must enter as fully as possible into the essence of the flower or the tree. Isamu Noguchi, the Japanese-American sculptor, chiseled as little as possible in his later days so as to "let the stone speak." Basho, who got so much of Japan into so few syllables, makes the thought as accessible as any Asian ever has in one of his poems:

From the pine tree
learn of the pine tree,
And from the bamboo
of the bamboo.

Henri Bergson put a Western gloss on the point in *Introduction to Metaphysics*. There are two ways to know a thing, the French thinker wrote: One can walk around it and observe it, or one can enter into it by way of intuition and sympathy—"an effort of imagination." This latter was the idea the Japanese had of themselves in nature. It was Basho's point. And we need only look at Japan today to understand what happened. The old notions were not precisely erased—not altogether. But there was no attempt to reinterpret them in a modern context. They were, instead, museumized. They existed side by side, a little schizophrenically, with the idea of nature imported from the West. And this is why the nation that trains its pines and bathes in volcanic springs has also covered itself in concrete—expressways, urban sprawl, immense factory compounds, hydro-electric dams on every major river in the islands but one.

What was to remain Japanese as Japan left Asia behind? The short answer among the Meiji oligarchs appears to have been "Not much." But certain things endured. *Nihongo*, as Japanese is called, of course kept its place. So did the old idea of belonging: One was Japanese not because of any plebiscite but by way of birth and blood. Power can thus be said to have remained Japanese, too, in that the state enforced this notion of belonging. It is common, also, to assert that the Japanese aesthetic is purely, brilliantly Japanese. But this is not entirely so. Certainly the Japanese fertilized many Western imaginations. But Western modernists—Frank Lloyd Wright comes immediately to mind—just as certainly influenced what we think of today as the Japanese aesthetic.

If *datsu-A* left the Japanese one legacy more than any other, we would have to name it a truly extraordinary state of confusion. With all the erasing and forgetting and burying came—another paradox—a kind of suppressed obsession with all that was lost on the way to modernity. This nostalgia still runs deep. It is part of what it means now to be Japanese: to long for the lost, to pull at a few remaining threads binding the erased past to the present. The primitive pottery, the old dance, the architecture identified with the ancient period: The taste for these becomes a kind of secret subversion of Japan as it has made itself. "All art, all true culture, is made by outsiders," a noted dancer named Min Tanaka once said in conversation. We were sitting under a tree on a farm, where Tanaka insisted that his students cultivate vegetables in the morning before dancing all afternoon. Tanaka danced *butoh*—"the dance of darkness," the ancient Dionysian dance from the tradition underneath the tradition.

As to the rest of Asia, Japanese thinking became impossibly convoluted as soon as Japan made to depart. Leaving Asia turned out to mean colonizing Asia, beginning with China in 1895. Japan honored all it had learned from Asia, so to depart from Asia was to depart from itself. But it needed Asia as it left because it had to conquer Asia to prove, Western-style, it was superior to Asia. It would colonize, but it would learn well from the West on this point. The colonies were about protecting Asia from the Western wind: This was Japan's version of *la mission civilisatrice*. The mission made Japan an "other," as all such missions do, but in this case the other became an other to itself. In the end the convolution came to this: Japan would save the past to destroy it and—the paradox is monumental—destroy the past to save it.

DATSU-A WAS NOT AMONG the slogans the Japanese held high in making a modern nation. Fukuzawa wrote of it only once, although once seems to have been enough. So we must follow the thread, for it runs a length. Another noted thinker of the Meiji period, Nitobe Inazo, famously declared that Japan should make itself "a bridge over the Pacific"—a kindly interpreter of the East to the West and the West to the East. Okuma Shigenobu, a count and one of the prominent political figures of the late nineteenth and early twentieth centuries, thought Japan must stand for "the harmony of Eastern and Western civilizations." Only a few years ago a longtime politician and the prime minister at the time, Yasuo Fukuda, asked the rest of Asia (and the Americans) to join in making the Pacific "an inland sea." All such ideas roll off the spool set in motion by a brief opinion piece penned in the mid-1880s.

It is all well meant or it is all neurotic—and it is fair to wonder which. After the war, when the Japanese could do only what the Americans told them to do, Fukuzawa's *datsu-A* became *datsu-A, nu-O*: leaving Asia, joining the West. In the 1980s and 1990s, as Japan became rich, trade friction rose, and American power began to look less convincing, the thoughts evolved and multiplied. It is a discourse lost to most Westerners, but most Japanese are familiar with the phrases:

NU-A, DATSU-O: joining Asia, departing the West

NU-A, NU-O: joining Asia and the West both

NU-A, SHIN-O: joining Asia, being merely friendly with the West

The most recent of these thoughts is the most drastic since Fukuzawa's day: *Zai-A, shin-O* translates as "being Asian, being only friendly with the West." Being Asian, or "existing in Asia" (another translation), is a considerable leap. Is Japan at last prepared to declare itself what it has been all along? Is the confusion about to lift? Is the destruction of history about to end?

OVER MANY YEARS I enjoyed a friendship with a Diet member called Satsuki Eda. He was in his forties when I met him, in the late 1980s, a modest man with keen eyes and a quick intellect. Eda headed a small party that held a half-dozen legislative seats and was well regarded on all sides as an evenhanded commentator—a kind of one-man Greek chorus amid the commotion of Tokyo politics.

Eda and I spoke often over many years—sometimes in his Tokyo office, sometimes in Okayama, his home city in the southwest. Eda was waiting for something. He saw Japanese politics as a series of stages. Meiji had brought the nation-state: "But that was a palace revolt and didn't involve many people." There was 1945: "We established a democratic system, but people were not ready to activate the system." And there was now, now being the early 1990s: "Now we're at a third stage. People are still not accustomed to voting on their individual views of things. They vote out of belonging—to a family, a community, a company, a union. But they're learning. They're preparing to operate a system for themselves." This seems now to have come to pass: Eda's party came to power not long after I last saw him, signaling a new maturity among Japanese voters.

Over time I began to see that Eda, whether he knew it or not, was turning Ernest Renan on his head. Making a nation requires some forgetting, but in our time it is not the forgetting Renan had in mind. One must forget not the facts of history but, at least partly, the old way of belonging. And with a new way of belonging comes the capacity not to forget history but to remember it properly.

This is essential if Japan is to cure the neurosis of history that began with the idea that it could leave Asia behind. It is important to Japan but just as much so to its neighbors. If the

nineteenth century was the West's and if ours belongs as much
to the East, remembering what is to be remembered and forgetting what should be forgotten will be fundamental to Asia's
coming-of-age.

It is well enough known that the Japanese have stammered
and stumbled for most of the postwar era over their apologies for the events of the Pacific war. Japan, and especially official Japan, has not known how to remember this period.
Approved textbooks have long reflected an abiding ambivalence: There had been wrongs, but not all Japan did was wrong.
The imperial Japanese went out to civilize, to make Asia one, to
make it something that could withstand the Western wind; *la
mission*. Has any nation, fair to ask, ever apologized for its old
mission?

But something happened in the mid-1990s. It was around
the time Eda sensed the coming of a new idea of belonging and
(no coincidence) in the years after Hirohito's death in 1989.
One practically felt in the air that Japan was bracing to articulate itself anew. And the moment came in 1995, on the fiftieth
anniversary of the surrender. The prime minister at the time
was a Socialist named Murayama Tomiichi. His time in office
was brief; he was a well-intentioned but ineffectual figure. But
Murayama stood up in the Diet that August 15 and said this in
the matter of "colonial rule," "aggression," and the "suffering
and damage" imperial Japan had inflicted on Asia:

> I regard, in a spirit of humility, these irrefutable facts of history,
> and express here once again my feelings of deep remorse and
> state my heartfelt apology.

A decade later Junichiro Koizumi, a prime minister of far
greater stature, pointedly repeated some of these phrases. The
occasion was another fiftieth anniversary—this of the Non-
Aligned Movement at Bandung, the Indonesian resort town
where it had been founded:

> Japan squarely faces the facts of history in a spirit of humility.
> And with feelings of deep remorse and heartfelt apology always
> in mind . . .

These were decisive moments—moments of history. They are comparable to Willy Brandt's "Warsaw genuflection," that occasion in 1970 when the German chancellor knelt and bowed before a memorial to the Jewish ghetto. That was a transforming act for Germany and its neighbors. Japan, by contrast, enjoys no such credit. Asia's sensations of weakness and victimhood first arose from the encounter with the West. But they were transferred onto the Japanese in the mid-twentieth century. Their notable apologies have not proven enough for the simple reason that an unapologetic Japan remains more useful in the Asian neighborhood than an apologetic Japan. Many Asians, notably the Chinese, simply do not seem psychologically prepared to do without the props and hurts of victimhood. But the steps have been taken—toward what the Japanese like to call "a normal nation," toward the condition they now term *zai-A*, being Asian again, which is to say remembering themselves again after so long forgetting.

There is an irony in the prospect that Japan will at last master memory and with it the imported machine called the nation. The mastery will come just as the twentieth century recedes into the past and as nations begin to look like the technology of a passing era. Of all that Renan may have thought we might forget, could he have imagined that we may someday forget the nation itself? The Japanese raise the question somehow—perhaps because they seem more keenly aware than the rest of us that an ending appears on the horizon, however distant. People will have to learn to express themselves by way of other technologies: The Japanese are attentive to this for the simple reason they were never at home with the machinery of the nation in the first place. "Sovereignty grows weaker, border walls lower," Satsuki Eda once said in conversation. "The nation-state isn't the absolute rule of human beings—nothing eternal. It's the product of a certain age. It'll go on for a time— thirty years, forty—but in our century this will change, too."

3

SITES OF MEMORY, the thinker who invented the term tells us, are "where memory crystallizes and secretes itself." Connecting memory to places goes back to the Greeks, who counted remembering among their arts. Orators memorized speeches by identifying passages with parts of a building, which they pictured in their minds as they spoke. We use places and objects today in somewhat the same fashion. Museums, monuments, rooms left as their occupants had them: These are sites of memory.

There are many sites of memory in Asia, despite all its ripping down and reinventing. The peace park in Hiroshima, with its famous remains of the domed building destroyed by the atom bomb, is such a site. Tuol Sleng in Phnom Penh, the Khmer Rouge execution center, is another. But as an imperative to remember, for its dedication to memory as an eternally required condition of consciousness, nothing in Asia matches the Nanjing Memorial Hall. Neatly enough, China divides in two in these matters: There is remembering China and there is forgetting China. This makes China, without any question, the weediest of all Asia's memory gardens. Nanjing shows us one way China remembers.

Nanjing was China's capital when, in December 1937, it fell to Japanese troops. Six weeks of executions, rape, looting, and arson followed. The casualty figures remain a question, but there is much to suggest that the Chinese count, 300,000, is credible.

The original memorial to the Nanjing massacre opened in 1985. There were thousands of artifacts, photographs, military maps, documents, diaries. At the core lay a narrative and a chronology: These were the events, this is how they unfolded, and we in the present look back upon them. There was an implication of distance.

All of this is now known simply as Phase 1. Phase 2, completed in 2007 to mark the seventieth anniversary, is a different kind of place. It is seven times the size of the original. One elevation is lined with bronzes depicting various victims—orphans, oldsters, a mother with a dead child, a bespectacled professor fleeing with his wife. The captions for these are bluntly emotional; several refer to the Japanese as "the devils." Along another wall the figure 300,000 is written in twelve languages. In the exhibition halls one is assaulted by every visual, video, audio, and lighting effect, every kind of *tableau vivant*, now available to curators. A murmur of mourning is now more nearly a shout of accusation.

The most curious feature of the new museum is the way one is required to go through it. The architecture defines a sequence, and one cannot easily deviate. There is a public archive of victims' histories, a mass grave discovered during construction, the exhibition halls, then a "peace park," then a meditation hall (dark, illuminated by candles floating on water), then a wall of names, and finally a graveled square, each gray pebble intended to commemorate a victim. The whole is enclosed, like sacred space, by high walls of black stone.

The museum's architect was named He Jingtang. He kept his offices in Guangzhou, where I visited him the next time I passed through the city. He was a lively sort, engaged and engaging, distinguished but also accessible. I mentioned the severity of the museum's granite and marble, the absence of color amid the blacks and grays, the enclosing walls, and the way one was required to go through the place.

All this was by design, He Jingtang explained. Every visitor is to make a journey—from war to peace, from death to life, from past to future. "This isn't a building," he said as we stood over a model under a glass case. "It's a place of astonishment. It's a shock. We put so many walls in place to isolate people once they enter—to achieve the sense of compression we wanted. Once within, one can see nothing of the outside world."

As a technical accomplishment, He Jingtang's memorial deserves admiration. The power of the site—in its lines, shape, and color, in its stark stone—is evident when one glimpses it several blocks away. And in its assertive claim not only on our minds and emotions but also on our bodies and our participation, the Nanjing memorial achieves its purpose, perhaps even triumphantly.

But what do we think of its purpose?

Social memory, the recalling of the past in a given way because we belong to a given group, is how we remember many things. We do not preserve the past so much as reconstruct it—an essentially social activity. This is what we mean when we use the term—too often too loosely—"collective memory." And it is with collective remembering in mind that we must question so forceful a site of memory as Nanjing. This is essential to understanding what the memorial does to the visitor. The distance and chronology of an ordinary exhibition—we are here, the events back there—have been eliminated. We become complicit, the population of a rite; in a certain way we are performers in an acted sequence.

There are many kinds of forgetting in China—a reality familiar to anyone who knows the Chinese or their modern story. There is forced forgetting, pretended forgetting, genuine forgetting, the forgetting of never having known—forgetting as erasure. Nanjing suggests the same about memory. It is an example of coerced remembering: One will not only remember the massacre but also remember it in a certain way, and one will remember with a certain response—an emotional response.

And to remember this way is essential, according to the architects of memory, to being Chinese.

A heavy spring rain was falling when He Jingtang and I finished talking, and he offered to take me to the gates of the university where he kept his studio. He was leaving himself, he said, to make a trip to Shantou. This was a remarkable coincidence, for I, too, was planning to take the brief flight to Shantou the following day. There is not much to the place. It is a coastal city and one of the special economic zones China designated during Deng's years. But it had lost out to the others. I had but one reason to go: Outside of Shantou was the only museum in China dedicated to the Cultural Revolution. I had wanted to visit for a long time.

I told He Jingtang of my plans, and our conversation shifted. He was in the front seat next to his driver, and he turned half around as he spoke.

"I, too, suffered during the Cultural Revolution. But we ought not fixate on that era. We have to see it in the proper context. We must reevaluate events that came before according to where we are in the present."

With this, He Jingtang turned forward again and gazed out at the rain.

"Still," I persisted, "to see Nanjing and then find so little given over to the Cultural Revolution."

He Jingtang continued watching the rain. "Oh, that," he said, waving his hand back toward me. "Those sorts of places are here and there—small rooms in museums about other things. There are several in Sichuan, I've heard."

He paused. Then: "It's like Nanjing, I suppose. It must be remembered. Those events are thirty years in the past, thirty years of our development, and I suppose we should examine them. But it's wrong to dwell too much. In the end it's different from Nanjing. There are still Japanese who deny it happened."

He Jingtang seemed finished, but I decided to go on.

"Remembering and forgetting," I mused. "It's always interesting to find what each nation is supposed to recall well or not recall at all."

He Jingtang turned suddenly to face me as far as his seat belt allowed.

"Why are you so preoccupied with that time?" this gracious man snapped.

We just then reached the university gates.

BEFORE THE REFORMS, most of China looked like Shantou today—gritty, stuck in the rusted ambitions of the Communist period. Much of China still has this look, we ought not forget, but Shantou is especially unappealing. It is tired—tired even of itself, even amid all the adrenaline one finds elsewhere. But the Cultural Revolution Museum, hidden within a country park some miles out of town, has drawn me back twice since I first saw it. It is a site of memory where there is supposed to be no such site.

I always called the same driver in advance of these journeys. His name was Liu Dajun. He was born in the 1970s, and he had none of the prickly sensitivity of He Jingtang. When we first met it was midday, and I took Liu to a lunch of beer and bowls of noodles before setting out. He was not the least curious that I had come to see the museum.

"Have you been before?" I asked.

"Once or twice I've driven people."

"And what did you think?"

"I wasn't terribly moved one way or another," Liu replied. "Besides, it all happened to another generation."

I mentioned that I had been to the memorial in Nanjing. At this, Liu looked up from his noodles. As with most Chinese, to utter the name "Nanjing" was enough, and he had a strong opinion about the incident. And as with most, for Liu it came down to what scholars call a national-character argument, the kind of argument made at the Nanjing museum: The Japanese did this because they are Japanese, and this is what Japanese do.

Liu said, much as He Jingtang had said, "These are very different things. One is an international matter, one nation to another. The other is between us. It's like a family. In a family, disputes can be settled quickly, can't they?"

Over time my talks with Liu changed. He told me about the memory of various generations: Those older than forty-five had strong memories of the Cultural Revolution; those thirty-five to forty-five had "some memory of it." Younger people had no memory, Liu said, and his own was "weak."

Liu also talked about his family, and the story grew more interesting. Many more people than he had suggested earlier had their memories. But these were handed down from parents and uncles to children and nephews and nieces, and they were unspoken memories, understood within a household but rarely raised. They were privatized memories. Part of Liu's memory came from his name. "Dajun" means "great soldier," and his grandfather had wanted Liu to be one in the People's Liberation Army. But there were other memories. Liu came from a family of intellectuals. "Three of my elders were victims. They were all sent to the countryside. There's no need to speak of it. This is not just my family. It's the story of a generation."

PENG QI'AN, WHO FOUNDED the Cultural Revolution Museum, designed it, built it, and in 2005 opened its doors, had memories, too. He had been a county official when the events began in the 1960s. Then came denunciations and public humiliations—three hundred of them before it was over: Peng was called a capitalist and went on a local list of "enemies of the people." When he got out of prison after three years, he counted himself "a lucky survivor."

But Peng did not build his museum out of any sense of animosity or personal injury, so far as I could make out. He had gone to Ta Shan, Tower Hill, the forested park outside Shantou, in the mid-1990s. He found a mass grave and asked around. Yes, the villagers said: seventy victims. Some time later a friend sent two books published in Hong Kong. In them Peng read of Ba Jin, one of China's honored modern writers. Ba Jin was famous during his last years for an essay calling for a museum, a place to remember the events of the decade that ended with Mao's death in 1976.

"I hadn't heard of Ba Jin," Peng said. "I'm not an intellectual. But when I read about his dream, I thought, 'Why not? Why not something that will keep us from forgetting?' "

Peng was in his midsixties when we met, a tall man with thin hair, without elegance but with great dignity. He wore a plain gray shirt, light trousers, and cheap sandals. We talked in the main hall of the museum, sitting on plastic chairs and sipping tea poured from a pot on the floor beside us.

Peng had raised sixteen million yuan, about two million dollars, to get his museum built. It was a strange-looking place, halfway between a rotunda and a squat pagoda. Peng had taken the plates from the books published in Hong Kong and had had the pages engraved on tablets of black garnet. There were hundreds of them mounted around the hall, each filled with text and pictures. They presented a precise chronology—month by month, year by year, event or decision or trial or proclamation by event, decision, trial, or proclamation. As you went around the hall, you walked through history—a walk as Nanjing was a walk, but without the coercion. It produced, instead, a sense of revelation. There was cause and effect, human agency. One was asked to think before one felt.

"My thought was to create good history for later generations," Peng said simply.

I wondered aloud how such a thing was possible. When I had first telephoned the city offices to get the museum's address, a municipal official had hung up on me. I mentioned this, and Peng smiled. It turned out that officials in Shantou had been of many minds when Peng began his project. No, there would be no funds from the city. But the city could give money for roads and public buildings at Ta Shan, and if they went toward the museum, they went toward the museum.

"What about Beijing, then? Surely that was a different story."

It was, and still more interesting.

Peng said: "They found out about it just as we were opening. Two officials from the local propaganda department were sent to investigate. A couple of months later a city official came to see me. He said, 'Don't wait for any response from the central government because no one from the party or any party committee will have anything to say about your museum, good or bad. It'll be an unfinished answer from here on out—eternally.' "

CHINA THINKS OF ITSELF by way of generations: The "50ers," the "60ers," the "70ers," and so on. The decade of one's birth comes up more or less continually because it reveals what you recall, forget, have been taught, or never knew. This reflects the shocking mutilation of Chinese consciousness during the Communist era and since. You can talk to octogenarians about the Long March and Mao's caves at Yan'an. Those now in their twenties—the "80ers"—are not clear even about the Tian'anmen incident in 1989.

Memory and forgetting, then, make a précis of China's past century. It suggests the price China has paid for its incessant abuse of history since it replaced past-consciousness with future-consciousness. It explains a numbness many Chinese have developed, even among those who have suffered: the numbness of He Jingtang's flick of the hand, my driver's flippant remarks as we ate our noodles in Shantou. Beneath the numbness lie a billion lakes of private memory. They are there among the ambivalent party officials as much as among ordinary people. They make secret sites of memory. And among the most honorable tasks a Chinese can assume today is Peng Qi'an's task: the bringing of these stilled lakes to the surface, the stirring of the water.

SIDE BY SIDE, the museums in Nanjing and Shantou mark out China's affliction with history. Nanjing suggests a need to remember victimhood more or less eternally. Japan's original sin was *datsu-A*, its daring declaration that it was leaving Asia, and then treating China as an inferior "other." As to the neurosis of forgetting, beneath it lies not only numbness but also an inability to feel sorrow. Sorrow requires forgiveness, and the Chinese are yet to forgive themselves, most of all, for their self-inflicted wounds. The Anti-Rightist Campaign, the Great Leap Forward, the Cultural Revolution, Tian'anmen: These cover more than thirty years of the Communist era and its aftermath, each one a disaster. The sin yet to be cleansed is how blindly so many Chinese followed. For all the avant-garde political rhetoric, they had still not made themselves modern. One looks at pictures of the shouting, frenetic crowds on the walls of Peng Qi'an's museum: The faces are those of people who understood belonging not much differently, we can fairly suppose, from the Qin dynasty's subjects.

A FEW WINTERS AGO A SMALL, frail man with an impish smile published an essay that lit a fire within the Chinese leadership. It flickers to this day. Xie Tao was no minor deviationist, as the party might once have put it. He was eighty-five when he presented his critique of Communist rule; he had joined the party at twenty-five. He had been purged and then, in 1980, "rehabilitated." When he published his essay, he had recently retired as vice president of Renmin University—People's University— one of China's most honored institutions.

"Political reform can no longer be delayed," Xie had written. "Only constitutional democracy can fundamentally solve the ruling party's problems. Only democratic socialism can save China. Poverty is not socialism; affluence and corruption are not socialism, either."

I wanted to meet Xie. There are political tendencies galore among Chinese intellectuals and party officials, and it was not my intent to explore another of them. Xie had done something different—not merely because of what he said, but also because of who he was. Xie had argued from within. He advocated what he called the Nordic model—the socialism of western Europe. This was Marx's socialism, Xie had argued. In political terms he had used the Second International to attack the Third—the Comintern, the socialism of Lenin. So it was Mao who had deviated. The error had begun in Moscow, and China had followed the wrong road. All this from a man who had breathed the air at Yan'an, walked in and out of the famous caves, and borne the young Mao's message out to the rest of the world.

It said something vital about China's modern history. It suggested the diversity to be found in the recent past, even amid the commotion of the interwar years, a fertile commotion, and even as the Communists rose amid the post-Qing confusion. It made one marvel at how much had been lost and how close China had come to an alternative future—a future that could be more than merely an endless extension of the present.

XIE TAO HAD RETIRED to Chengdu, his home city in Sichuan. I took a train down from Beijing the autumn after his essay had appeared, just as a big party congress was concluding. We met at a teahouse and ended up talking for two days—in restaurants, on drives through the city, over dinner in the apartment he kept with his wife, a Russian-speaking psychologist who also remembered the old days at Yan'an and the early days of optimism after Mao had gone to Beijing.

Xie was eighty-six by this time, yet his features never lost their animation, as if they reflected a kinetic mind ever making connections. We spoke of many things. Yes, we Chinese once thought of the Soviets as our friends and the Americans as our enemies, he said at one point. In the next sentence he recalled the enthusiasm he and his young Communist friends had felt as they read American writers: Steinbeck, Hemingway, the black novelists, Pearl Buck. I felt in the presence of what amounted to historical evidence. Complexity: This was the quality of Xie's mind, the thing the revolution had erased in so many other minds. In this way Xie was erasing an erasure for me to reveal something that had been long hidden.

"Remember Mr. Democracy?" he asked.

I told him I had an interest in the idea.

"We never finished learning from Mr. Democracy. No one could think during the Maoist years. He made himself the brain of the whole nation. Mao gave us the era of lost expression."

"What about the Deng period, then?" I was thinking of Xie's resurrection and rise to a top post at a prestigious university.

"Deng gave us the era of lost memory," Xie replied. "Nothing can be mentioned. Nothing of history can be discussed. This is China's biggest struggle now—or one of them: to speak, to put history back in our newspapers and our media."

Old men with old Communist credentials are untouchable in China today. Xie had written, and the ripples had stirred across the stilled surface, but how much more could be said? One had to be old, and one could say it once. I put the thought as delicately as I could.

Xie minded not at all.

"You have to read the words that brought you here as symptomatic," he replied. "You look below the surface and you find a gradual process. At this point you can see it even at the top. Look at the party congress they just concluded: no mention of Mao, start to finish. We're headed for a complete reexamination."

One hears this often in China—very often in conversing

with young people and the younger party functionaries: Look beneath; something else is coming. This is how Asia changes. It is among the things Eda-*san* in Tokyo taught me. Change often emerges after a long period of silent, invisible germination. One learns to trust the notion—and to ask how long a given change will take to make itself apparent.

"It's thirty years since the reforms began," Xie replied when I put the thought to him. "In another thirty we can achieve this."

WE CANNOT DESCRIBE the impulse to remember, as Xie Tao displayed it, as rampant across China. It is something closer to incipient, or imminent, or inchoate. All the reinventing going on at such extraordinary speed is immensely destructive. The wiping out of cities is part of the wiping out of memory. If your building, your city block, and your neighborhood are all gone, how difficult will you find it to remember and how easy to forget? Change of the kind China's leadership has chosen leaves the Chinese marooned in the present. But it begins to produce what it is intended to erase: a desire to find that usable past we all must seek. People must remember, first, how to remember: such is the depth of the damage during the Maoist years and the years of Dengist forgetting.

Peng Qi'an told me he had a half-million visitors a year at his museum outside Shantou. Given what I saw and with simple arithmetic, I could not be certain this was so. But one has to watch only one or two groups going through: a pair of parents pointing at the plaques and leaning over their children to explain, a schoolteacher with forty charges touching the tablets with their fingertips. It is enough, such that one cannot quite look into Peng Qi'an's face for a moment or two. In a nation of a billion forgetters, he is passing on the act of remembering.

Making memory into history is the work of professional historians. And China's historians are now in something of an uproar. Everyone knows that to determine the past is to determine the future, and China—official China—no longer knows what to think or say about the past. History departments all over the country are alive with talk. What is taught varies from place to place. Methodology—theory, the conduct of research, the use of documentation—is unfixed, the object of contention among numerous schools. We must count this confusion as progress. One can teach more or less what one wants, professors will tell you. Approach the invisible borders of the permissible and an older professor will be sent to inspect your lectures and approve or "correct." It is what one puts in writing that is subject to hard-going official scrutiny. This is the scrutiny Yuan Weishi came in for.

Yuan Weishi was in the mold of Xie Tao: old enough to write of things as he saw them. He had published an essay called "Modernization and History Textbooks." It first appeared in a small magazine called *Dongfang* (Eastern Culture). Later it was reprinted in *China Youth*, a national newspaper. And it was then that Yuan had lit a fire of his own. The piece had come out in a column called "Bing Dian" (The Freezing Point), meaning roughly "subject to debate." The column never again appeared.

Yuan greeted me on a rainy Saturday at the apartment he kept on the campus of Sun Yat-sen University in Guangzhou. He was a courteous but reserved man with silver hair. Yuan's strategy in his essay was interesting. He had taken two incidents in Chinese history and followed accounts of them in textbooks. One was the burning of the Summer Palace by British troops in 1860—fallout from the Opium Wars. The second was the Boxer Rebellion of 1900. Textbooks explain the first incident as the unprovoked barbarism of foreigners. In accounts of the rebellion, the Boxers were heroic proto-revolutionaries, and foreigners, once more, were "foreign devils."

Yuan's essential question reminded me again of Xie Tao: Where is the historical complexity in these accounts? Where are the explanations of the Qing court's mistakes in provoking the palace burning? Where is the description of the Boxers as compulsively antimodern and antiforeign? Where are the

Boxers' barbarisms? "These are facts everyone knows," Yuan had written. "Yet our children's compulsory textbooks will not speak about them."

Yuan discussed all this at some length. "This is our inheritance," he said in a tone of restrained anger. "We're still in the nineteenth century. History texts remain completely irrational. People compiling them regard everything China does as right. Later on, everything about the revolution was right. Now everything about the Communist Party is right. This is contrary to the research of many historians. Remembering properly is the required path of turning Chinese into modern citizens. Modern citizens must have rational thoughts."

I did not know how to read Yuan Weishi's case. He had published, so prompting conversation all over China. In his apartment he recounted the incident without self-consciousness. But Yuan had been erased, in the end. And the textbooks he attacked, after all, were still in use. What could one take from this?

I knew a historian in Xiamen, the coastal city once called Amoy, who had studied the decades before the revolution—Xie Tao's youthful years. The professor's name was also Xie, but he was not related to the old, delightful socialist in Chengdu.

Xie Yong called his study *Lost Universities*. He divided prerevolutionary China by generations—how else?—and looked at how each had been educated. The earlier generations had had the last of the traditional system—a master, rote learning, heavy emphasis on the classics. Later generations had been schooled in a more purely Western fashion. Those in between had had a mix of methods. Xie Tao would have been educated in this middle way: He had acquired his English (long corroded by the time we met) at a missionary school. And it was this mixed group that had shown the best result: "liberal minds," as the professor in Xiamen put it—able to grasp an imported idea but attentive to China as it was.

"This is what came to an end in 1949," Xie Yong said as we talked.

Xie Yong was somewhere in his forties, which made him a "60er." And he had written *Lost Universities* partly as a historian and partly as someone overcome by the thought of a China he had never known. His "lost universities" were his critique of China as it had come to be—his elliptical equivalent of Yuan Weishi's blunt essay. Schools stood for the press, the way culture was produced, ideas hatched and official policy made, the way books were written and published—all that made up "the knowledge system," as Xie Yong put it.

"I have a nostalgia for what is missing," he said. "You'll find this prevalent among the intellectuals. There was a liberal space in those years. It was possible for people to mature—an individual maturity. Now there's no such personal space. It causes serious problems."

At this, our conversation shifted to the present.

"You see an ever-degrading quality in Chinese thinking since 1949," Xie Yong said. "The knowledge system is one-dimensional because it's all controlled. The other problem is personality. The personality does not form properly. And people can't express themselves truthfully—only in private is this possible, as I'm sure you know already. Dishonesty becomes a pervasive trait."

Xie Yong sipped tea. When he spoke again, it was once more in the generational vein.

"Only in the '80ers' do you see anything different."

"Why the '80ers'?"

"They've grown up in a slightly different environment and they've forgotten so much."

"But, Xie Yong, surely forgetting is a chronic malady, a blight."

"There are two sides to it," Xie Yong replied. "The '80ers' have little knowledge, and sometimes none, of something like

the Cultural Revolution. They have no way to judge its importance. So they ask about it. They begin to talk and write about
it. They know no better. This is why the official forgetting we
are supposed to do will not produce the desired result. People
forget why they are supposed to forget, and then they start to
remember."

In Beijing I knew another professor named Li Shaobing. He
was young, with a good position at a leading university, and he
was highly attuned to how the managing of history was changing. Li taught me much over our conversations—some at Uncle
Wang's teahouse near Tian'anmen Square, some in coffee-
houses near the campus where he lectured. I asked Li once
about written records. I had found the same sensitivity to the
inscribed, as against the spoken, in other Chinese societies.

"It's tradition," Li replied. "People of a given time don't
comment on their time. It's thought they can't be objective. It's
the people of the next dynasty who write about the previous
dynasty. The Ming wrote Yuan dynasty history. The history of
Ming was written by the Qing."

"Then this must be changing," I replied. "The Maoist
period is over."

"It's changing, yes. I don't think this can be prevented. But
there is one problem. It is the same dynasty. This is still the CP
dynasty."

THE "CP DYNASTY," as we now have it, has a complex relationship with history, to put the point too mildly. In the reform era
it wants the Chinese to remember things it is ideologically
committed to making them forget and to forget things it is
equally committed to keeping in their minds.

The party's current slogan, to be found in any given edition
of *People's Daily*, offers a good example. It is *hexie shehui*, "harmonious society." This is not unlike the old credenda in Meiji
Japan, a simply stated way to go forward. And it is historical
allusion in a very pure form, understood by all Chinese. "Har-

monious society" is a barely veiled entreaty to follow the teachings of Confucius. But the great Kong Fuzi will rarely be mentioned, if ever, in any party document or any piece in *People's Daily.* The Confucian tradition was prominent among Mao's "four olds": It had to go. The message in each repetition of *hexie shehui* thus achieves the very zenith of paradox: Citizens will please remember what we have instructed you to put out of your minds.

There are Confucian experts, revivalists, reenactors, priests, acolytes, and general purveyors of the tradition all over China today. They receive no official support, so far as one can make out. But the government is plainly enough happy to have them around. The narrative of the revolution is dead, and as the party promotes "harmonious society" as a less-than-stirring replacement, the new Confucianists are useful even if they cannot be openly encouraged. Mao's future-consciousness—utopia lies ahead—is changed, not back to past-consciousness so much as to a consciousness of an ever-extended present: Utopia is now; this is it. Let us find something of ourselves in the past so as to be happy in our harmonious heaven.

There is a Confucian temple in central Beijing that was undergoing an extensive restoration a few years ago. It dates to the fourteenth century: It was where Yuan dynasty candidates for the imperial bureaucracy took their examinations. The Ming rebuilt it; the Qing then added a lecture hall where the emperor held forth on the classics. Yuan, Ming, Qing, CP: four dynasties, four iterations.

I used to go to the temple on Saturday mornings. I once came upon a crowd of boys and girls, primary-school age, as they flocked behind a man in black silk robes. The children, too, wore robes. Under them one could see the striped gym trousers and running shoes that are the standard gear of any middle-class Beijing child. Behind them, arms crossed, were rows of pleased parents and, in folding chairs, rows of grandparents.

The man began bowing before a rosewood altar set in front of a statue of the great sage. The children followed in (dis)harmonious imitation, as best they could. Then the man spoke and the children dispersed, each approaching his or her grandparents. One by one they bowed.

"What is the lesson?" I asked a mother standing nearby. She was of early middle age, beaming at the scene.

"He is an expert in etiquette, with seven years' experience as a teacher. The children are learning form, procedure."

I asked to meet the expert with experience. His name was Shen Ziqiang, which comes into English, curiously, as "Self-Strengthening Shen." And it turned out he worked at something called the SSL Cultural Development Company. It had publications, a training unit, tours for people in search of their cultural roots, a health-and-happiness program, and a forum to promote Chinese tradition abroad. Shen was silent as the chief executive, a young efficient sort, explained all this.

"What is it you teach, Mr. Shen?" I asked when the CEO was done.

"I wouldn't say I'm a teacher. I'm a practitioner of etiquette and ceremony. There are two aspects to Confucian teachings: what is written, the texts, and then the ceremony. You can see posture and movement in the ceremony. These are the expression of the values."

I had met numerous neo-Confucians, and always it was the same: They knew next to nothing of *The Analects* or any text that had followed down the centuries; the preoccupation was form, protocol, behavior, the how-to-do-it of the tradition. This was not a new story. The history of Confucianism is in part the history of its vulgarization, each generation using it to address its need. I put the thought to Shen as politely as I could. To my surprise, he did not disagree.

"I teach people with rules," Shen replied. "In a society that changes so fast, people need to find a place we can call home—a place of belonging."

Shen paused. Then he grew expansive.

"In thirty years we've achieved much. But with gains come losses. We can't find our roots. We're like a kite without a string. It makes us a nation made of anxiety."

Can the Confucian revival we now witness across China be counted as a search for a usable past? Or is it merely a retreat from the chaotic present, a desperate gush of nostalgia? Classical Confucianism concerns the defining of relationships. One is identified by way of one's place: father or son, husband or wife, elder brother or younger, ruler or minister, friend and friend. Only the last is free from hierarchy. All five of the orthodox relationships are exclusionary; none admit of individual subjectivity. The only way to make the tradition modern is to strip these features of the thinking out of it. But the result can no longer count as Confucianism by any ordinary idea of it. What remains is nearer to a guide to good manners in a society so raucous and devoid of values it has lost the habit of them.

We must appreciate the difficulty of the endeavor facing each individual Chinese. To become modern, to belong in the new way, to reinvent the self: In a society that lived so long by precedent, these undertakings are precisely without precedent. This is why being Chinese has been so peculiarly provisional for the past century and more. But this can be neither cause nor excuse for flinching, which is what Shen Ziqiang, for all his native intelligence and honesty, advocated. A usable past does not permit an escape into it.

THE MING GAVE US BEIJING as it has come down to us—even if swaths of it are now being destroyed. They made it a circular city, a city of concentric walls, moats, and ring roads, and within the innermost of these they put the Forbidden City and, just outside it, the vast, flat approach—Tian'anmen Square. This was in the early fifteenth century, when Beijing became, we think, the world's largest city for the next two hundred years.

There is nothing like the center of the Central Realm anywhere in Asia. It is sheer semiology, a set of signifiers. The old imperial place is a museum, of course. One enters through Tian'anmen, the Gate of Heavenly Peace, above which hangs an immense portrait of Mao. Opposite the gate, ranged around the square and the avenue bordering it, are a number of buildings—an interesting collection: Mao's mausoleum, the Great Hall of the People, a museum to the revolution, the Monument to the People's Heroes, and then the Ministry of State Security.

All this is emphatically public: It is display. Within the palace grounds, the Forbidden City remains forbidden. Of what we know of Mao's later years, he spent them there much as Wanli spent his as the end of Ming approached: indulging his appetites, reading the classics, refusing to see his officials. Now as in Mao's time, the Forbidden City houses institutions more powerful than any presented outside, apart from the police: Here is the party's central committee, here is the State Council. None but the modern mandarins see these. To look at this arrangement of sites is strange when we think of modern Chinese history. The Communists came to destroy the old, and yet their claim to glory is refracted off the old like sunlight off a mirror.

Above it all hangs a picture of a man much loved for getting China finally to stand up—no one can fail to see this among the Chinese. But Mao has become, as the past seeps into the present, a figure no one particularly wants to talk about, not even at party congresses. He is the diametric opposite of Confucius: Recall the sage, even as we have told you to forget him; put Mao out of your minds, even as we tell you to remember him. A silence now enfolds Mao: Let us all honor the Helmsman, even if he has left us speechless. The man who began so much of China's forgetting makes his way, ever so gradually, into the ranks of the forgotten.

THE TRAIN TO YAN'AN climbs through barren country, dry and steep. Roads, terraces, hilltops, walls, dwellings—they are all carved from the soil, giving the land a little of the look of Middle Earth. In Yan'an, people have lived in *yaodong*, caves dug into the hills, for many centuries. It was in such caves that Mao made himself Mao, taking control of the Communist armies and preparing to take Beijing.

How is Mao remembered in the place he dwelled during his most heroic years? The question seized me at dusk one winter's evening as I crossed before Tian'anmen and, bent against the wind and rain, looked up at the famous portrait.

Yan'an turned out to be another exercise in CP dynasty semiology. Along the gravel path leading up to the historic caves, there was a shop selling souvenirs, sundries, and ice cream. Out front, facing the walkway, was a television screen playing a video at maximum volume. It was a narrative of the Gang of Four—Jiang Qing, Mao's wife, and the three other "ultraleftists" blamed for the Cultural Revolution's excesses. There was a long story of how they had sought to hijack "New China." It explained how they were cornered politically and then arrested. It showed footage—evocative, this—of the trials. It was, altogether, an instruction manual for forgetters: the extravagantly inaccurate story of how Mao's China was saved from the errors of a few and had gone on to remain Mao's China. I watched until I was satisfied the tape played in a continuous loop, over and over.

The caves, set beneath a brow of craggy hills, had vaulted ceilings, brick floors, and whitewashed walls. Mao's was the biggest, with meeting rooms and photographs of the smiling Helmsman "and his family," neither wife nor daughter getting names. The other caves were but two rooms each. Here was Zhou Enlai's bed, washbasin, and bookcase. Here was the table where Zhu De, the brilliant military commander, spread his maps. The place was not monastic so much as compellingly austere. It exuded the idealism of the early years, which is why "Red tourism" holds an attraction for some Chinese.

An older lady from Xi'an was on her third visit. Her father had been arrested as a "rightist," and she had been sent "to live in a cowshed," as she put it. "But mostly we remember the good things because we're much better off now." There was a man from Hubei, a province to the east. He had come with his work unit and seemed full of the old spirit. "We're here to memorialize the revolutionary past," the old man said with vigor.

In front of Zhu De's cave there was a stone table with a bench on either side and a chessboard that had long ago been painted into the surface. At it sat a man in his forties. He wore a quilted coat stained with grease, and he needed a shave. It was either his careless appearance or the way he stared vacantly into the middle distance that made me sit and begin talking. His name was Wang Yijiang. I do not normally take an interest in the meaning of Chinese names, but this one possessed a poetry I found hard to resist: Translated and Westernized, Wang Yijiang was One River Wang, and that was how I knew him that afternoon at the caves and over the dinner we shared in town that evening.

He was a "6oer" and was from Changsha, an industrial city in the south. Too young to recall anything of the Cultural Revolution, he could only study it as best he was able, given the meager materials available. But he remembered the Tian'anmen incident vividly. It was his crucible. One River had helped organize demonstrations at Changsha University. Then he watched them fail, wrote obligatory letters of "self-criticism," and began to do what many of his generation did after 1989: He drifted, first into retail work, then into occasional jobs when he needed them. One River had a motorcycle, and with it he wandered. He had come to Yan'an as I had, to see how people remember. His next journey would be to Tibet.

"I'm just a tourist," One River said with a shrug.

I took his word on this point. He meant it: He was lost in a world that would not remember with him. It left him contemplating Tibet "because it's there." It left him gazing into space at Zhu De's chess table.

"The Maoist era was a disaster, Tian'anmen an idealistic passion with no plan or organization," One River said. "It's not that people don't remember. They can't. I have friends who were with me in 1989 and then went into business—a common story. Even when we see one another, we can't talk about it. You either have hope or you go numb."

One River had not gone numb—his blessing and his curse all at once. It had left him alive but alone. And yet he seemed, in his odd, misshapen life, a life that could go neither forward nor back, to stand for so much of what I have seen in China: In him was distilled an immense wistfulness.

History, as Pierre Nora has written, is the enemy of memory. As I have seen it and think of it now, to record the past is to shed the burden of remembering within ourselves. This is history in the service of life, as Nietzsche put it. Forgetting of a desirable kind becomes possible; we are capable of living in the present—carrying the past but not borne down by it. To neglect history, then, is to let the past haunt us, to imprison ourselves with the imperative always to remember. This was One River, claustrophobic within his memories, with no history to bear them away. And One River seemed to articulate what many silenced millions could not.

At dinner that evening, at a tourist hotel in Yan'an, One River said the thing I knew would print him in my own memory.

"We're all like sand in a river being washed away. We can't look back. One of the weaknesses of the Chinese nation is that we cannot admit our weaknesses."

4

ON A CLIFF OVERLOOKING the Arabian Sea, across from the
Strait of Hormuz and the Persian Gulf, there is a temple that
counts among the most historic in Hinduism. Every Hindu
knows Somanatha, or knows of it. "Somanatha," a Calcutta
matron replied when I mentioned it one evening over dinner,
"I must go before I die." That is Somanatha for many Hindus.
It is a kind of Mecca, though this expression would be other
than appreciated.

It is interesting to see Somanatha on maps drawn before
national boundaries were. It was almost as close to Baghdad
and Kabul as to Delhi or Calcutta or Madras. It was part of
another world, the world of West Asia, a world that had little to
do with India as we now think of it. When Somanatha was first
built, we think in the tenth century, trading traffic across the
Arabian Sea was already dense. This trade, centered on coastal
towns such as Somanatha, eventually extended across Central
Asia and into China. It made this part of India rich. The mark
of these centuries is still evident in Gujarat, the state where
Somanatha is located. Gujarat's population—90 percent Hindu,
10 percent Muslim—still shares Gujarati as its common language. Its merchants are still known (the world over now) for a
clever hand in business.

What people know most about Somanatha is that it was
looted many times and eventually destroyed. Temples such
as Somanatha liked the trade because they prospered, too.
Traders from various places respected one another's faiths and
traditions and, indeed, sometimes adopted them. This produced, quite early, the syncretism one often finds in this part of
the world. "To you, ye gods, belongs the merchant!" Schiller
once wrote. So it was in Gujarat. With commerce flowed
knowledge, invention, and ideas in many directions. But with

the traders came various raiders. They preyed on the temples and on the pilgrims going to and from them. For a long time travel was treacherous; piracy at sea remained common until the nineteenth century.

No one knows how many times Somanatha was raided. Nine times, twelve times, twenty times: I have heard all these figures. The most famous raid occurred, by the best historical evidence, in 1026. It was executed by a sultan named Mahmud of Ghazni. Ghazni is a city in present-day Afghanistan, about midway between Kabul and Kandahar. Mahmud's kingdom extended westward into what is now Iran and north into Central Asia. It was a restless power in its part of the world.

Mahmud seems to have been, indeed, an ambitious man. He wanted his capital to be a center of literary culture and the arts. Mahmud was also a dedicated Sunni and an evidently savvy player in the politics of West Asia. He was, most of all, an accomplished marauder. Raiding was a typical way of amassing wealth in Mahmud's time—limited not at all to Muslims to the north and west of what is now India. Mahmud looted entire libraries so that scholars would come to Ghazni to study. He attacked treasuries and many temples to pay for his court life and his mercenaries. In all of this, Mahmud was not especially discriminate. He attacked non-Sunni Muslims as well as Hindus and others. At one point he gave command of his armies to a Hindu named Tilak, who seems to have served with the utmost loyalty.

We do not know precisely what Mahmud did in 1026. He may have destroyed the temple, or he may merely have desecrated it. He may have killed many people—fifty thousand by one unlikely account—and he seems to have got away with an immense amount of temple wealth. Most important, Mahmud destroyed the idol in the temple's inner sanctum: He burned it, broke it and left it, stole it, shattered it and took some of the pieces to Ghazni. Again we are not certain.

Who was the man who attacked Somanatha? Once more, it

is unclear. He was a warrior gathering wealth. He may have wanted to disrupt the horse trade across the Arabian Sea because Ghazni was losing out, so he could have been a commercial man in this sense. He smashed the idol, but this is complicated: One of the ancient historians explains that the idol was thought by some to be Manat, a pre-Islamic goddess condemned by the Prophet. So Mahmud may have acted as a Muslim at Somanatha, but we do not know if the mission was to destroy a Hindu idol or one worshipped by heretical Muslims.

Histories of this event began appearing not long after it occurred. They are tangled, full of hyperbole, impossible numbers of people, and different amounts of gold and jewels. The idol was a lingam, a stone phallus, some accounts tell us; no, it had human features and was covered in gems. The temple was stone; the temple was teak. Mahmud's motive was this, it was that, it was the other.

Romila Thapar, one of the great historians of her generation in India, recently produced a book unraveling all these stories to the extent even a first-rank scholar can. I have drawn some detail from it and from Thapar's lectures. The book is not a history of the temple: That was long ago lost to history's mists. Thapar's study is a history of all the histories, and her thought is that we learn more about the teller in each account than about the story as it is told. "What is remembered is that which survives, even though it has been chiseled anew in each retelling," Thapar notes. "Perhaps some events are forgotten but recorded, and the record becomes another memory."

How does Somanatha come to us in our time, then? What need is answered by the narrative we have today, the story implicit in the "twelve times" and "twenty times" that one hears across India?

Somanatha remained a ruin for many centuries. At the site today one small part of the old temple remains, a plinth that appears to have supported a cluster of columns. It gives a strong suggestion of the size of the place: an imposing structure as it looked over the Arabian Sea. The remaining stones are discolored, and one can see where the salt of the crashing tides below ate into them, just as the old histories said it did. Look closely at this block of intricately carved stone and you find many suggestions of influence in its weathered-away figures and patterns: possibly Hellenic, possibly Roman, possibly Persian, possibly Arabic. Bearing the chronology of many centuries, it is a small site of memory.

But this is not the fate of Somanatha. It became, instead, the site of a reconstructed history. And the way this reconstruction has occurred has turned Somanatha from a site of memory into a site of false memory, fantastic memory, memory in the service of creating a new idea of India and of Hinduism. All of which is to say Somanatha is now a site of forgetting.

NOT LONG AFTER independence a group of politicians took up the idea that Somanatha should be rebuilt. A new nation needed a new symbol—a sign to all that it would remake itself and reclaim its former greatness. One of those leading this procession was named K. M. Munshi, a former writer of historical fiction in which the idealized glories of the Hindu past never failed to figure. Munshi seems to have been an aggressive propagandist for whatever he wished were so, and he let it be known that it was the new government that was rebuilding the temple. The president, Rajendra Prasad, then agreed to officiate at Somanatha's reopening ceremony. Diplomats abroad were asked to collect water from the rivers flowing in their assigned countries, that these could be used in the celebratory rituals. "For a thousand years," Munshi wrote, "Mahmud's destruction of the shrine has been burnt into the collective subconscious of the race, as an unforgettable national disaster."

We should pause over this thought, bearing in mind Renan's old warning about the confounding of race, religion, and nation. Munshi's "race" was the Hindu race (which is not by any definition a race). Munshi's unforgettable disaster was a "national" disaster—a disaster for India, teem as it may with races, religions, and ethnic groups. With perfect hindsight we see in this the tragedy of many things to come. Nehru was incensed by all this confounding and quickly drew a line under it. The new temple was financed by a trust unrelated to the government. But the founding father won only an early battle in a war that continues, often a lot more gruesomely, into our time.

The Somanatha project began in 1951. So it took India but four years to begin its erasures. A certain kind of nation began to disappear almost as soon as it came into being. India had survived for many centuries much as the Gujarati traders had. It was not that there were no differences among people but just the opposite: There were so many differences that "difference" could not be made to matter. There were Ghaznavid traders in India and Indian traders in Ghazni. Among so many "others," otherness becomes of no use as a way of organizing one's world.

To many Indians this will seem a contentious account of the past in too few words. But it is how we must describe the India that began to erase itself soon after it became India. Tolerant, syncretic living began to give way to separate living. Otherness became the very drum around which one's life spun. It was a retreat, almost instant, into the old belonging, as if the new belonging—"I am now an Indian before I am anything else"— were either too much to manage or not enough to sustain one's identity.

This was why Somanatha rose again in the early 1950s. With it came a new narrative—clean, simple to understand. The race and nation would be the Hindu race and nation. The twelve or twenty times: There would no longer be any ambiguity as to this. Mahmud was not a marauder in need of money. He was a Muslim, a Turk—a term still used oddly often among Hindus— and the Turk has done this to us, we Hindus, we Indians.

Somanatha appears against the sky long before one reaches it. The first thing one sees is the sandstone-colored dome, then the roof over the many-columned antechamber, then the immense stone entrance. Inside begin the numerous appeals of the trust that built and still maintains the place. "Let us restore the golden age of Somanatha," reads one signed by Shri Keshubhai Patel, the trust's chairman. There is an appeal to donate toward a new guesthouse. And then this one, which mentions parts of the temple:

> The historical accounts reveal that Aadi Jyotirling Somnath Temple was decorated in gold and jewels. Shree Somnath Trust is making humble efforts to restore the ancient glory by gold-plating the surface of Nij-Mandir and Sabha Mandap. Devotees are invited to join hands at this historical and noble project. You may drop your donations in cash or kind or cheque or . . .

And so on: an appeal to the pocket and to participation via one's need to know that history will be served—history, the instrument by which an identity and an idea of nationality are constructed, the past as determinant of the present.

The temple today, not quite six decades after its rebuilding, seems to remain a work in progress (just as history ever is). The architecture is a vulgarized version of the Hindu style—a little Disneyesque. It was the people I found interesting. Most were devotees, milling about in family groups in the temple and around the grounds. In the anteroom people would suddenly drop to the floor, foreheads to the marble tiles, and recite incantations. Many others seemed—as those of a certain generation used to say—blissed-out. And still others were aggressively joyous, even defiantly joyous. At the door leading to a garden and a promenade near the sea, some teenage boys pushed their faces into mine and, eyes wide and glassy, shouted, "Somanatha is very great!" This is not, to put it mildly, the ordinary behavior of Hindus at temple.

At the seawall I wanted to see something called the South Pole Indicator. It is nearly as famous as the temple itself. It is a painted globe atop a column with an arrow piercing it, pointing due south. Beneath it an inscription explains: "The light path stretching without obstruction up to the South Pole over the end of the ocean." The globe carries some totemic meaning. It seems to validate Hinduism as a religion of universal worth. Sitting on a bench and studying the thing—crudely carved, crudely painted, crudely explained—I could register none of this. Yet my mind went back to all the Hindus I had known who had urged me not to miss the globe at Somanatha. "You'll see," my matronly friend in Calcutta had said. "It proves it: Hinduism is for all the world."

I lingered until evening. There was a *son et lumière* show projected onto the temple's rear wall. And it was as I had expected. Erased was any idea that we sat in a place with a many-layered history, the complexity of India as it is. Nothing of a people given to confluence and the habits of syncretism. A short distance along the coast were Persian inscriptions dating to 1301, marking a place where Mahmud was said to have built a shrine. But from our small grandstand we watched a tale of primary-school simplicity, good versus evil, the eternal invulnerability of Hinduism.

I WAS ONCE TAKEN to a temple in the north of India that was, my local acquaintance thought, about four hundred years old. It was small but well proportioned, with an intricately carved dome. In the dim light inside I could make out murals—birds and animals, deities, human figures, patterns—painted into the plaster walls and the ceiling of the dome. They were vividly colored, having never had much light, and they were done in a style that was primitive but also splendidly modern. One could see traces of folk traditions that were not at all Hindu. Anywhere else and the work of a painter laboring in the sixteenth or seventeenth century might have earned a place in a museum.

And then, as my eyes explored, something else: Here and there the dome was leaking. There were water marks on the plaster, and some of the colors had run. I began to spot small growths of moss. When I expressed concern, neither my companion nor the caretaker showed the slightest interest.

This is Hinduism in our age, an age of decline and the corrupting of things. Temples, along with everything else, deteriorate in such an age: This is a matter of acceptance, and acceptance—of the general falling apart of the world in the long age of Kali—is part of traditional Hinduism. One finds temples like the one in the far north across India: dilapidated, left to themselves, littered and unswept. Carelessness comes in the age of Kali; the salt that decayed the stones at Somanatha and the raids of Mahmud were so accounted for.

Some years ago an Indian thinker named K. J. Shah posed some questions about Hinduism. Is it a religion or a philosophy? Is it both? Is it both but one more than the other? His last question was his best: "Who knows what Hinduism is?"

Shah's point lay in what he asked, for there are no answers. There is an absence of structure in Hinduism that makes definition impossible. Hinduism has no book, no Bible or Qur'an. It has no Vatican. There are practices but no laws. We count the gods in the hundreds of thousands, each village or town or hamlet on the plains or in the mountains having its own. One cannot go from one part of India to another and practice one's Hinduism as at home, because the gods will all be different. Hinduism is what one makes of it. It is too inclusive—another traditional characteristic—to be otherwise. It is receiving rather than projecting. It is less a faith than a way of life, a friend once observed. One could neither agree nor contradict with certainty.

The Hinduism of carelessly kept temples and countless gods, the uncodified faith without much by way of edges, is the Hinduism that came down to India across many centuries. Some Indians tell you that its multiplicity is what inclines India toward its traditional openness to strangers, an at-homeness with others. But this is not the Hinduism of Somanatha or any of the large, new temples one finds around India today. That is another, more recent idea. In my notes I took to calling it "neo-Hinduism."

At its extreme this new Hinduism is called Hindutva. Hindutva is not much more clearly understood than Hinduism, for there are numerous versions of it. It is neither religion, nor philosophy, nor faith. It is an ideology, one with a relatively brief but very interesting story.

Traditional Hinduism, it can be said, possesses a certain greatness precisely because it makes no claim to greatness. In its informality and its lack of ambition for itself lies a liberal space that marks it out from other religions (if we count it a religion). The new Hinduism turns this on its head. It makes extravagant claims to greatness. It is assertive rather than recessive, projecting rather than receiving, and exclusive rather than inclusive. Instead of any liberal space, one finds a closed space, a space of self and other.

This is the Hinduism of Somanatha. It aspires to the things of a great religion—a clear tradition, grand churches, truths as against myths and legends, a book as Christians, Jews, and Muslims have their books. The book remains unresolved, for there are many books in Hindu tradition. But a little in the way of Christian fundamentalists, works once read as literature and metaphysical reflection are to be read as historically accurate narrative.

From such beliefs and aspirations it is but a small step to Hindutva ideology. As a matter of shorthand, we can think of this as political Hinduism as one speaks of political Islam. India is Hindu, the Hindu self the true Indian self. The rest—the teeming, populous, cacophonous remainder—this is a vast erasure, for none of it is truly India.

The appeal of the new Hinduism has been evident for several decades. In 1977, when Congress was voted out of power for the first time since independence, the coalition that replaced it was much influenced by Hindutva ideologues. These same ideologues subsequently formed the Bharatiya Janata Party, the BJP, and took power directly in 1998. Before and since, the "we" and "they" of the new Hinduism has grown ever more apparent.

We know the inflammatory power of this narrative of separateness by way of a great deal of highly publicized communal violence, notably in Gujarat. But we ought not miss the more salient point: Something lying between neo-Hinduism and Hindutva is prominent, if not prevalent, in India's middle class. You find it in court judgments and faintly fascistic temple architecture and in the conversations you might have with a business executive, a scientist, or an otherwise ordinary university student. Hindutva or a variation of it, we cannot be surprised to learn, is widespread among the technologists in Bangalore and among the NRIs, nonresident Indians, in California and New Jersey. Those most modern are often most in need of the past Hindutva offers them.

The past as it truly was is a burden for neo-Hindus and the adherents of Hindutva. One does not find in it a place for a purely Hindu India. The paradox is that a kind of past-consciousness reigns among neo-Hindus. It is on the skein of the past that the present is to be painted. And so India as it was must be forgotten and an India that never was "remembered."

How did this come to be? How could a nation gifted with so singularly diverse a history come to forget itself for the sake of a few facile simplicities? How have so many in it come to erase the richness of the past in favor of a past that can never be truly remembered because it never occurred as they wished it had? The answers to these questions are theme and variation, for we find behind India's impulse to erase and fabricate the same induced self-contempt noted elsewhere in modern Asia.

In the name of pride, self-denial; in the name of identity, an abdication.

ONE OF THE MOST INFLUENTIAL BOOKS in modern Indian history was not written by an Indian. Neither did James Mill think it necessary to visit India, speak any Indian language, or know any Indians when he sat down, in 1806, to begin *The History of British India*. He preferred, he explained when he published his three volumes a decade later, the detachment of a jurist. Among the curious features of *The History* is that it did not, at its core, concern India. Mill had England and English politics foremost in his mind.

Mill was a utilitarian, a follower of Jeremy Bentham. The worth of a thing lies in its usefulness: This was Bentham's philosophy in brief. All people, cultures, practices, and human endeavors could be so evaluated. We need not dwell on definitions because, as previously suggested, we are perfectly familiar with the utilitarian method, two centuries on from its formulation: It remains the way we think, not least when we think about Asia. But at the time Mill wrote *The History* the utilitarians were just forcing their way into the English conversation. Their adversaries were conservatives such as Edmund Burke and eighteenth-century romantics such as Rousseau, who advanced the noble savage and the simple life then being lost to the beginnings of the modern. Mill's purpose, then, was to apply the utilitarian philosophy to India, where England's role was then much in debate, to demonstrate its efficacy. Mill opposed colonization because it was inefficient. Indian courts and schools should proceed in Indian languages: This was more useful.

Mill left his mark on India by way of two methods. He had a peculiar distaste for the past. There was not much to be salvaged from India's, he considered. He discounted all thoughts of greatness in any previous era of Hindu history; the subcontinent, in his view, should be approached as a kind of tabula rasa. In the original edition, Mill gave but two dozen pages to the past of the Hindus. "Rude nations seem to derive a peculiar gratification from pretensions to a remote antiquity," Mill marveled. "As a boastful and turgid vanity distinguishes markedly the oriental nations, they have in most instances carried their claims extravagantly high." So much, then, for Hindus before the British found them.

The History also divided Indian chronology into eras. Scholars say it "periodicized." Mill described a Hindu era, a Muslim era, and a British era. This had not been done before. And there is next to nothing in Indian history to suggest that so dividing it was, to take Mill's word, of the least utility. Muslim influence came to India by way of trade centuries before the Mughals came to rule. These centuries wove an intricate carpet, incrementally and informally and made by many million fingers. Out of this came one history. Rarely did either a Muslim or a Hindu rule solely as a Muslim or a Hindu. For a long time the British were considered simply another caste. Much of this was lost in Mill's "periodicizing." We can illustrate the point by way of Mahmud's raid on Somanatha: Only in the nineteenth century was this made a trauma suffered by Hindus. By then, it was useful to understand the past as a matter of supposedly old antagonisms.

The Muslims were militant, despotic, and given to fierce fighting. So they had been in the Western consciousness since the Crusades, and so they were described during the period of Mughal rule in India. What of the Hindus, then? They were, by contrast, inferior in nearly all ways—an enervated, degenerate people with fantastical myths but no history, wanting in social structure and institutions, ungiven to science. Next to the Muslim the Hindu was weak—inefficient, ignorant, timid.

"The attention of the Hindu is much more engaged by frivolous observances, than by objects of utility," Mill wrote in a typical passage. Elsewhere he noted "this listless apathy and corporeal weakness of the natives of Hindustan" and "the languid and slothful habits of the Hindu."

Two years after the publication of *The History of British India*, Mill was named to a senior position at the British East India Company, which then managed England's interests in the subcontinent. Mill remained there for the rest of his life, and his famous son, John Stuart, followed him into the business. The book went through many editions. It was standard reading for company officials and, in time, for civil servants during the Raj. Mill's thinking became mainstream thinking. One still finds traces of it in the offhand remarks many a Westerner will make today.

It is possible to exaggerate the impact of Mill and his caricatures and his periodicizing; many Indians do. Mill did nothing single-handedly. But the orthodoxy he helped create had its influence, for Indians came to contemplate as fact what their subjugators said was so about them. And it was amid their deep feelings of failure and inadequacy and the slights of history that Hindus had their first reactions against the orthodoxy. These came in the 1870s, among intellectuals from the educated elite. If all this was wrong with the Hindu, they said, then the Hindu would have to think again.

HINDUTVA DID NOT GET its name until 1923, when a nationalist named V. D. Savarkar asserted from a British jail that for India to be a nation, it would have to be a Hindu nation. But we can trace Savarkar's thinking back to the decades after the end of the British East India Company and the beginning of the Raj in 1858. These were the years Japan and China were formulating their responses to the arriving West. The circumstances were different, but in India as to its east we find the familiar themes: nostalgia, weakness, *ressentiment.* Hindutva, even be-fore it was named, sounded all of them.

Among the ideology's earliest inspirations was a devout believer named Dayananda Saraswati. Dayananda had been born into a Brahman family and had studied to become a Hindu priest. Then his doubts got the better of him. There-after he wandered, proselytizing for the top-to-bottom refor-mulation of a faith that was every bit the mess, he thought, that Westerners found it to be. Idolatry, mythology, local traditions and gods—all of this had to go. In their place would come the things of a proper religion: one god, no multiplicity of sects, and a book (the Vedas). Only then would Hindus overcome their degeneracy, escape foreign domination, and regain their lost golden age. In 1875, Dayananda started Arya Samaj, the Aryan Society. Half a century before Hindutva got its name, we can count it the founding of what is now the ideology's vast and virulent apparatus of organizations.

Dayananda had numerous heirs, each elaborating what be-came preoccupations. The Hindu was weak and wanting in virility: Too much time on the metaphysical plane had caused this. The Hindu was unscientific and must rediscover the sci-ence found in the Vedas: no place for "historical fables," as Mill had called them. Finally, there was the matter of the self. The Hindu must understand the world anew, for the world was made of the Hindu and the other. The Muslim and the Chris-tian were conquerors because they were manly and muscular and scientific. But they are only among us, not of us: The Indian self is the Hindu self.

It was Savarkar, the imprisoned pamphleteer, who took a faith and, having none himself, welded it into the ideology that blights India today. He loved and hated Muslims, not so oddly. He found their resolute valor "irresistible," he once confessed. But he needed Muslims more than he cared for them, for the Hindu self required an "other." This was a question of space as

well as "race." For Savarkar, India had lost its way the day Mahmud of Ghazni first went south across the Indus River. "That
day the conflict of life and death began," Savarkar once wrote.
"Nothing makes the self more conscious of itself so much as a
conflict with the non-self."

Savarkar was not—and this truly is odd—a religious man.
He was an atheist, by all accounts. Neither did he join what
remains the most powerful of Hindutva's numerous organizations, the Rashtriya Swayamsevak Sangh, commonly known
as the RSS. But he perfected the style we know today by way of
the RSS: a givenness to invective, hate-mongering, and revenge;
a compulsive consciousness of the utopia of the Hindu past and
Hindu victimhood in the present; a taste for violence as a form
of theater; an admiration for fascist imagery and methods. Hindutva borrowed heavily from the Europeans in cultivating an
idea of the nation. But it borrowed all the wrong things (and
from the wrong Europeans). Race, religion, geography—blood
and soil: These were what Renan warned against. But these are
what India's movement of Hindu nationalists chose, and we
have already witnessed Hindutva's frightening ascendancy.

INDIA NEVER SUFFERED a consuming angst in the matter of
spirit and things—not as Japan and China did. Only in recent
years has the arrival of new technologies disrupted its train
of thought. But it is useful to consider India's modern crisis in
the light of what we know of *ti* and *yong*, for it is another case
of theme and variation. Certainly India has had an enveloping debate over that most troublesome piece of modern
machinery—the nation-state. This was the form India's crisis
with the West eventually assumed. It has gone on for well more
than a century, and we witness this crisis still.

The principal lines of argument are familiar. Gandhi favored
independence, of course, and played an essential role in the
nationalist movement. But he advanced a critique of the nationalist elite and their imported idea of progress in everything he

did and with every sandal and sarong he ever wore. Tagore and the mahatma clashed, famously, over the question. To Tagore, nationalism amounted to nothing more than the worship of foreign idols. The nation simply was not enough to fulfill humanity's needs and realize its potential: It was "glass for the price of diamonds."

Nehru was the committed nationalist. He was the believer in science and Western superiority in all matters materially manifest. He was the one who would "invent India." But Nehru was a believer in progress as the West meant it—progress in sequential time. "India," as he conceived of it, was to be all. His nationalism was in essence imitative—a homogenizing nationalism imported from abroad. In this, oddly, it shared a certain feature with the Hindutva idea of the nation: It was borrowed.

Nehru's nationalist narrative held up but twenty years and crumbled for any number of reasons: corruption, unachieved ideals, economic failures, the first pressures of what we now call globalism and the prevalent fashion for neoliberal thinking. But, tellingly enough, among the first signs that the old narrative was about to fail concerned history. In 1977 the RSS took public issue with a textbook called *Ancient India*. The thing was blasphemous, the Hindu right declared. It stated that in ancient times Brahmans had been beef eaters—an unutterable thought in Hindutva circles: It was the Muslims who ate beef. More than this, *Ancient India* explained that the Aryan race, root of Hindu identity, was not native to the land south and east of the Indus but had descended from the north and settled. This was left-wing propaganda, so far as Hindutva adherents were concerned. A book burning ensued, and *Ancient India* became a cause célèbre. It was that same year that Congress lost power to the coalition through which the RSS exerted the national political influence. In the years that followed, erasure became policy, and the question of how one belonged in India remained unresolved.

. . .

IN THE DRY, desolate northwest, near the Pakistan border and the edge of the Rajasthan deserts, there was a village called Bukna where a murder had taken place. It had to do with caste. Bukna was a village mostly of Rajputs, an upper caste known in history as one of warriors. And a Rajput man had killed a *dalit*, a member of the caste once known as untouchables.

Afterward, the *dalit* families in Bukna—two dozen of them— fled and made a refugee camp in front of the district office about eighty miles away. It was a messy, makeshift settlement: tents of plastic tarpaulin and scraps of carpet, no running water, cooking fires in front of each family's tent. The *dalits* had been there six months when I met them, and they had no plans to leave until the district office gave them justice and another village where they could settle. Neither had yet come.

There had been a long dispute over land. The Rajput villagers wanted to run a road through the property of a *dalit* named Kohalabhai. There was a court case, and Kohalabhai won. Then the Rajputs began attacking his house. Tensions grew, and the *dalits* in Bukna asked for protection. A police detachment came but stayed only a few weeks. When the police left, nine Rajputs waited until one morning when Kohalabhai was walking to the fields. Then they killed him with sticks, pipes, and what are known locally as *dhariya*, sickles used in barley harvesting.

This was the *dalits'* story. I heard it over a long afternoon at the refugee settlement, mostly from a man named Jodhabhai, a brother of the victim. We had sat on straw mats in the sand under a canvas canopy. When Jodhabhai had finished, I decided to make the long drive to Bukna to hear the Rajput account of things.

Bukna sat amid a flat expanse of scrubby land. It had electricity but no running water: Water came from a pipe that ran from a river fifty miles away. On the sandy pathways through the village there always seemed to be women bearing brass pots of water drawn from the communal tank the pipeline fed. If they were Rajput women, they were in purdah—an old custom. If they were not, they were not, so far as I could make out.

I came to a shed, open along the side facing the path, and a group of Rajput men invited me in for tea. There were a dozen or so of them, and we sat on broad benches made of coarsely cut timber and woven straw, with pillows and rugs scattered around us. It seemed to be where the Rajput elders gathered. An old man with his head wrapped and a thick mustache, both in the Rajput style, began to talk. Bukna was a good village, he said. Everyone farmed, and there were two grain crops as well as a crop of grass for the animals. They had a good production of milk.

The old man's name was Kajaji Govadaji Rajput, and he wanted to talk mostly about water. This was Bukna's problem, as it is India's: But a third or so of the nation's farmers have irrigated fields.

"We depend entirely on the monsoon, and that is only July until October," Kajaji said. "The groundwater is too deep, so it comes up salty. And the government brings no irrigation. In the past some foreign people built check dams in the other districts, and now that's good farmland. But we were left out."

Check dams: simple barriers across streams and rivulets.

Foreign people: those from aid agencies.

I wanted to talk about the murder case, but each time I tried, Kajaji went back to the matter of water. Finally I said simply, "Tell me about caste in Bukna."

"The root of the thing is historical," the old man replied. "This place was part of a kingdom. The king gave the land to the caste of Patels. So there's a division. But we have a good exchange. We go to their houses and ceremonies and they come to ours. This is historic practice. My father and grandfather did it this way. We're only following. It's the same with the women. They've always worn purdah, so they wear purdah. They have separate places to meet."

"Are there any *dalits* in Bukna?"

A tall, younger man intervened. His name was Ganesji Naranji Rajput.

"There are certain other families," he said, "but very few. Four or five."

"I've heard that some have gone away."

Ganesji spoke again.

"There were families who migrated here to work in the fields, but this was temporary and they left."

At this, the Rajput men began talking among themselves. We had been conversing through an interpreter, and he leaned over to explain.

"The murder case is under investigation," he whispered. "This place we're in belongs to the leader of the accused, and he has absconded. No one says where he is. They're getting worried with your questions."

When the men finished talking, the old man called a young boy from the corner of the shed. He was shy and handsome, and his ears were ringed with gold bands, a half dozen on each ear, each band with a jewel.

This, the old man said, was cause for celebration. The boy was to be married that day.

I was astonished. Statutes addressing the question of child marriage extended back to the colonial era. It was not unheard-of, but it was rare to come across it. "And how old is our young man?" I managed to ask.

The boy was not inclined to speak. "He's ten," the old man said with a touch of pride.

"And does our young man have a name?"

Ganesji and the others began talking again among themselves, and soon it was plain I had posed precisely the wrong question.

My interpreter whispered again.

"We had better go. They're certain now you're from the district office."

I LEARNED NO MORE about the *dalit* murder. But Bukna left me with many questions—questions it was useful to ask anywhere in India.

Who were the Rajputs living in Bukna? To what did they belong? How did they understand themselves and their belonging?

They were descendants of Rajput warriors when faced with the Patels, a farming caste, and they were Rajputs in relation to the *dalits*. They were Hindu and they were family in the matter of the young boy's marriage. They were Bukna villagers in the case of the murder and the district investigation. Were they Indian? Yes, but only in a kind of negative field. They were Indian because India was supposed to bring irrigation, and India had not come.

And then the *dalits*. They did not like the caste system, Jodhabhai had explained at the refugee camp, and they accepted it only because it was forced upon them. But they had a strong identity. When they fled the village they had rented a truck, and all the *dalits* in the area had contributed to the cost. This was *dalit* solidarity, and I had seen it elsewhere: a strong idea of belonging, even if it was theirs by imposition. The *dalits* were Indian, too. They wanted protection, justice, and resettlement—all from India. They were Indian, indeed, more than they were villagers or anything else. They had gone to the police, then to the courts, and finally to the district office. And there they sat, encamped with their smoking fires and improvised shelters in the middle of a bustling market town. But there they had to wait, for India, once again, had not shown up.

We can count seven notions of belonging in the story of the Rajputs and the *dalits* from Bukna. This is India. This is the nation Gandhi seems to have understood better than Nehru, for the founding father never seemed to take sufficient account of so many persistent kinds of belonging. To call Nehru's nation a mosaic is to use a worn cliché, but one searches for a better term. "Jigsaw puzzle" might do. It is not simply a question of a great multiplicity of social, cultural, ethnic, and religious identities; it is also a matter of multiple identities within each person and each community. To what does one belong and at what moment? In this respect, we know the population of the nation called India, but we do not know how many people can be called Indian. Many fewer, we must assume, than 1.1 billion. If a non-Indian is someone who does not know India, a friend once said, then there are many non-Indians in India.

The mosaic is, practically speaking, infinite. One cannot render either its vastness or its variety. One can pick up shards and examine them and hope to finish, if such an exercise can ever be called complete, with some small inkling of the whole. It is the elephant's tail approach, but, as follows, it must do.

JAIPUR, THE CAPITAL of Rajasthan, is known as the Pink City because the ruling maharaja painted the entire place said color to honor the coming of the Prince of Wales in 1853. The palace, the old fort, the Albert Museum—all this makes Jaipur a must-see on the route of what Indians call maharaja tourism.

I knew a woman named Kavita Srivastava who ran a kind of halfway house in one of the residential neighborhoods. People would come on no notice, stay however long they needed to, and then go back into their lives again or begin new ones. It made a kind of controlled chaos of Kavita's house. A couple of miles from the tourist sights and you passed from "Incredible India" to invisible India. This was another India altogether— an India of enclosures and of people trying to escape them.

There were Vimalesh and Ravi, she a Brahman, he a *dalit*,

both from a village a couple of hours' drive from Jaipur. They were young teachers. They had known each other from high school, and after a tortured courtship, full of angst about their castes and families, they had married: a Hindu ceremony, then a civil certification. At first they kept the marriage secret and continued to live with their families. Then, when both were away at teachers college, Vimalesh's family found out. There were efforts to force them apart. The Brahmans in the village began attacking Ravi's family. There were legal complaints and an armed confrontation at the police station. When Vimalesh lost her second child, to dengue fever, her family never offered any word.

When I met Vimalesh and Ravi, she had been dispossessed, and he had lost his job at a government school. She no longer considered herself a Brahman. "If I'm asked, I say I'm a *dalit*," she told me with an obstinate pride. In the village there was an uneasy peace, but they could never return. If they did, it would be to honor killings.

To exit the extended family in India is a complicated matter. How did they feel?

Vimalesh wore the red stripe of the married Hindu woman. She said, "I've done something different. I'm certain of my choices."

Ravi was thinking as Vimalesh spoke. He wore jeans and an open-necked shirt and seemed strikingly poised. He had nothing of the diminutive bearing one sometimes finds in *dalits*. After a moment he answered my question, with the same air of determination as his wife's.

"I've learned to live on my own, to put it in the simplest phrase."

CASTE REMAINS POWERFUL in India, plainly. But this varies from village to village, from town to town, and especially from city to countryside. In many places it is losing its traditional social force; there is more mobility in such matters as employment. Caste is becoming, instead, a political force. One of the rising parties in India is the Bahujan Samaj Party, the BSP, a party of *dalits*. And as its power accumulates, something interesting is occurring: Those of higher castes are joining. So as a political phenomenon caste produces a complex landscape.

Caste is complicated for individuals, too. If one is a *dalit* and succeeds in life, does one fight for *dalit* rights? Or does one move to a large city and obscure one's origins as best one can?

In Delhi I met an orthopedic surgeon named Yadu Lal. Lal's family were *dalits*, his father a maker of sandals. During his childhood they were much inspired by B. R. Ambedkar, Nehru's law minister and a famous fighter for *dalit* rights. Study at a missionary school opened the door to Lal's life. He earned a medical degree, and in 1984, at thirty-two, he was appointed a surgeon at a government hospital. A coveted fellowship in England followed. And then followed Lal's difficulties.

There were other doctors from lower castes in the government system, but none in high positions. Lal began to notice he was getting less and less time scheduled in the operating theaters. He charted the pattern and filed a complaint. Quickly enough, he was accused of incompetence during a surgical procedure and then removed from his post altogether. The case made headlines in the Delhi newspapers for many months. A judge eventually ruled against any charge of negligence, but Lal's career, when I met him, was in ruins. He was practicing at a small hospital without a sufficient supply of instruments to operate with any regularity—caught, this man, between fate and aspiration, born and made identities.

"It's a mockery of science," Lal said one evening in his home as he recounted all this. "In science we must analyze with logic. There has to be medical auditing. This is not the twenty-first century, this case. It's medieval India."

IN AJMER, ANOTHER CITY in Rajasthan, I knew a professor who taught at a convent school called Sophia College. Her name was Sandhya Raina. She was a sociologist, and she was a Brahman. Sandhya had stories to tell about her students and then, as our conversations proceeded, about herself.

Gender is another enclosure in India—another kind of belonging and another confinement. And it tends to be more enclosing the higher one's caste. I heard many stories at Sophia of young women graduating and then, within a few years, disappearing behind the opaque veils of a traditional Hindu marriage. One girl had written back to her professors for a time. She was from an upper-caste family and had finished at Sophia with honors. Then she went home, and her family put her to work tending the dairy cows. Then the letters trailed off, and no one ever knew what had become of the honors graduate.

I told Sandhya about Vimalesh and Ravi, whom I had recently met. She shook her head.

"Yes, there's more intermarriage now," she said, "but we're usually talking about castes close to one another. A Rajput and a Jat: There's not that much difference. But a Brahman and a *dalit*? This is an extreme case. Society will never approve of it—certainly not for the girl. No emotional support, psychological support, financial support, social support: Problems are inevitable if you are cut off from the family in India and society looks down on you."

Sandhya used the language of the sociologist. Marriage was endogamous in the caste system: One ordinarily married within one's caste. Ravi had married hypergamously—he had married up—and Vimalesh hypogamously, down. All this terminology was used, in the end, to describe a system Sandhya thought it important to maintain. She spoke from above it and within it all at once.

When we came to talk about Sandhya's life, she said, " 'Modern' means in our way of thinking, not in any way we dress or any such thing. Values vary from family to family. In ours we're modern in our outlook. I treat my daughter as an equal. But in the matter of marriage—this is too important. We can't leave aside our own culture. We can't be modern all the time."

———

MY CONVERSATIONS in Ajmer reminded me of someone I had once met in Hyderabad, a young man named Aravind Kumar. He was not so sophisticated as Sandhya Raina, but they resembled each other nonetheless. They both lived with a foot in the world we call modern and the other in a traditional world, the world typically called premodern.

Aravind had grown up in a town 150 miles from Hyderabad. His family was Maratha, which is classified as "BC," a backward caste, meaning a deprived caste. He took his bachelor's degree locally and in Telugu, the regional language. Then Aravind moved to Hyderabad to earn a degree in business. It was his first exposure to English-language instruction.

"Suddenly I had to improve my interpersonal skills," Aravind said. "Suddenly I had to meet corporate people."

I understood what Aravind meant. In Hyderabad he had to invent a new Aravind, a new self who could get along in an unfamiliar world full of unfamiliar people. And he seemed to have done well at it. The MBA brought work in an advertising agency and then a job promoting trade fairs. Aravind was full of the jargon: "conceptualizing the exhibition," "formulating promotional strategies," "marketing the venue," "on-site management." And one could see he loved it.

The job brought twenty-seven thousand rupees a month, six hundred dollars, and the twenty-seven thousand rupees brought Aravind's family—mother, father, siblings—to Hyderabad. He was looking after all of them in a house they rented. At twenty-seven, the new self and the old self coexisted.

"No thought of getting married, Aravind?" I once asked.

"Two or three years down the line I'll think about it. Even when I get married, we'll all stay together. But I want a love marriage, not an arranged marriage."

Aravind paused. Then: "Before I get married, I want a consensus in my family and her family."

"A consensus," I said.

"For me personally, caste doesn't matter. A person getting married should take the decision. Understanding between two people comes first, the wealth of families and all that later. But my mother is a very traditional BC. She hasn't been exposed. My father's the same."

"If you can't convince them, Aravind, will you marry in the same caste?"

"Obviously."

THE COMMUNAL VIOLENCE that tore through Gujarat in 2002 is well enough known and described. Much is the evidence that Hindutva groups had prepared in advance for the killings and the fires. They left scars on all of India. Afterward, a peculiar silence fell—a silence made of shock but also of desolation and shame. This is what India had come to? This is what India had made of Hinduism and Hinduism of India?

It was in the years after the violence that I met Nadeem Sayed in Ahmedabad. A friend in Bombay had given me his name, describing him in the vaguest of terms: a respected figure among local Muslims, a leader of some kind, but a leader of what was not clear. "He'll take you to meet the Imam at Jama Masjid if you ask nicely," my Bombay friend had said. Jama Masjid is among the most splendid mosques in India. It dates to the early fifteenth century, an immense sandstone structure with intricately carved columns—a mix, curiously, of Muslim and Hindu motifs.

Nadeem was gruff and hesitant on the telephone. What did I want? What would I write? Could I show him my other books? Then a pause. Then: "Be downstairs in your hotel in ten minutes."

He was somewhere in his thirties or forties, with his hair combed back in the style of Elvis. He had a motorcycle across the street, and on it we set out for the mosque in the center of the old city.

We began weaving in and out of the afternoon traffic.

Then, on a crowded avenue, Nadeem pulled astride another motorcycle. A woman, veiled and in black, was driving, with a cellular telephone in her left hand. And then something heart-stopping: At forty miles an hour Nadeem reached out and grabbed the telephone. For the next several miles, maintaining speed, Nadeem punched through the messages and numbers stored on the phone, the woman all the while driving closely and shouting. At a traffic signal, Nadeem finally allowed the woman to snatch back the telephone from his hand.

I said nothing. Nadeem and I, indeed, had only the simplest conversations over the course of our meetings—partly because we shared little by way of a common language and partly because Nadeem seemed to communicate with symbols and gestures. He showed me things and then left me to my conclusions.

We began winding our way through a series of narrow lanes and alleys. Some were paved, others made of packed earth. Open drains ran down the centers. Along these lanes: goats, dogs, chickens, children, idle men, men ironing clothing with irons heated on grills. I began to wonder where we were headed; we seemed to be backtracking our own route.

Then, suddenly, the woman with the cellular telephone reappeared down one of the lanes. We caught up to her, stopped, and words were exchanged. Was she a spouse, a sister, a girl-friend? I could not tell, and it did not much matter. Cellular telephones, it was well known, were powerful devices in traditional communities: They conferred autonomy, and no Muslim woman of any relation was to have much of this.

The Imam was a conservative man, opposed to television, women going to college, modern dresses, and (of course) cellular telephones. But he had no political inclinations, no animosity toward other communities. He was tall and thin, with a long silver beard. We sat on carpets outside his study, overlooking the mosque's vast central square.

"Imam," I said, "this mosque dates to 1424. For six hundred years the Islamic and Hindu communities existed with each other—side by side and together. And now there has been trouble."

"Six centuries ago our community had what I'll call character," the Imam replied. "Now this is gone."

"And the Hindu community?"

The Imam laughed.

"They, too. They also have lost their character. By this I mean their distinction, their morality, what made them what they were. 'Character-lose, character-lose'—it's this way for Muslims and Hindus both."

Our conversation drifted for a few moments. Then the Imam returned to our original point. "We are distinct now, but in a different way. And this is what troubles me greatly."

My time with the Imam was brief. Afterward, Nadeem took me back to my hotel. Again: a long, winding route, unnecessarily intricate, avoiding the city's thoroughfares but for when we had to cross one to disappear again into the lanes.

It took me some time to understand what Nadeem had shown me and what the Imam had meant. I had to learn Ahmedabad better before I could grasp it.

For a long time the city was a monument to India's tradition of tolerance and accommodation. It was founded in the fifteenth century by a sultan (Ahmed Shah, for whom it is also named). For many centuries afterward it was governed by Muslims. It was where India connected to the Islamic lands westward—South Asia to West Asia. Until recently the city's symbol was "the tree of life," a figure carved into the intricate window work of a sixteenth-century mosque. But all this was memory by the time I got to know Ahmedabad. It had become a measure not of tolerance but its opposite. It was a place where individual violence became mass violence, Hindu turned against Muslim. The tree of life was still there, etched superbly against the sky as one looked through its window. But it had been dropped as the city's symbol—because it was Muslim, as many Ahmedabad residents (Muslim and Hindu alike) would tell you.

With the partition of India, the British (and many Indians) made all the mistakes Ernest Renan had warned of. Ahmedabad was not immune from violence then, but neither was it the worst affected. Before 2002 many neighborhoods had been mixed. There had been instances of communal violence, but the technology had been more personal, if that is the word. Barbers' razors were the preferred instrument. There were many wounds, regrettably enough, but few deaths. And little in the city changed. It was the 2002 violence that brought the big change. It took on aspects of an ethnic cleansing. Razors were replaced by immense, well-fueled fires. Muslim women were gang-raped and then incinerated, as if old animosities and an old paranoia having to do with potency were being exorcised. There were many more deaths and more damage to the physical space of the city. Neighborhoods were cleared, and with them memory, and developers, property dealers, and builders effectively reengineered Ahmedabad. An integrated quarter of 150,000 people near my hotel had one Muslim family left in it. The rest lived in pockets. There were Muslim pockets and *dalit* pockets. And most of the city was Hindu and of the higher castes.

This is what Nadeem had shown me. In our drives through the Muslim slums he had shown me the remains of an erased city. And he had shown me that within the remains there was a law other than public, Indian law: a Muslim law. That was what he answered to and how he belonged. And that is what he wanted me to hear from the Imam: We are distinct now, as the Imam said, but in a different way.

I did not see Nadeem again for many months. I telephoned when I was back in Ahmedabad, traveling down to Somanatha. I told him my plans.

"It's an important place," Nadeem said.

"Is it? Why?"

"It's ancient."

"Ancient. Is that the reason?"

"It's very ancient," Nadeem said.

"It's just old, then."

Nadeem paused. Then he said, "History says Mahmud of Ghazni attacked there. Maybe more than once."

"History says it," I replied. "Is it true the way they say, do you think?"

Nadeem paused again.

"I don't know," he said after a long time. "It's all I can tell you: 'History says.' "

I WANTED TO MEET an RSS man in Ahmedabad. I had met members elsewhere, and always it was a similar story. India is Hindu, the rest are our guests—this delivered in the kindliest of tones.

But Ahmedabad was different. The 2002 violence had been concentrated there. And among the things that shocked India after it was the absence of remorse. I had seen this elsewhere—in Sri Lanka, for instance. Amid all the wreckage, murders, abuse, and disappearances in what amounted to a civil war, the same macabre silence prevailed. It reminded me, too, of some travels in China: India was quite different, but again, an inability to mourn.

I met Balakrishnan Parmar where he worked: in a dark, cavernous hall where he was training for the emergency-response medical service. He was twenty-seven, not long in from a district town called Himmatnagar, about forty miles distant. He was gangly and shy, a little perplexed at the sight of a foreign visitor in the training hall.

I asked Balakrishnan to tell me about 2002.

"That was an accident," he replied.

"An accident. Can you explain?"

"No, I can't," Balakrishnan said flatly. "We want to forget that incident. For one or two days there was violence. If you want to know about all that, ask an authorized person at an RSS office."

An accident: The planning had been highly sophisticated.

One or two days: The Gujarat violence continued in some localities for more than two months.

"Do you remember how it was in Himmatnagar? Was there trouble there?"

"It's not of any importance to study such matters."

Plainly, I had begun badly with Balakrishnan. So I asked him simply to tell me about RSS. He calmed and spoke more expansively.

"It started in 1925. The object was to make India independent. It wants to inspire youth for nationalism."

Balakrishnan had the date right but not much else. The RSS had taken an indifferent view of the independence struggle, preferring to cultivate "Hindu strength." So there was confusion—more erasing.

"A nationalist organization," I said with some surprise. "I thought it was a religious organization."

"Yes, it's a religious organization. Religion is the root of the nation. There's a difference between a country and a nation. A country is a land. A nation is the spiritual power of the people."

"The spiritual power," I repeated.

"Think about America. Everyone knows about politics. In India everyone knows about religion."

Our conversation continued in this fashion for some time. I was not surprised. It was boilerplate instruction in the RSS, full of blurred terminology and unresolved contradictions. India was Hindu and religion the root of India, but Muslims were religious, too. So were Jains, Christians, and so on. Religion is a matter of worship, but in India it is dharma—a kind of moral inevitability. Dharma was a Hindu idea, but everyone lives the dharma. But there was no single definition of dharma.

And there was no making sense of Balakrishnan. The more one sought clarity, the more tangled it all became. This goes back to the beginning of the RSS. As an ideology, Hindutva had always been something of a bowl of noodles.

Balakrishnan had joined the RSS in his hometown when still in his teens. He became part of the local *shakha*, a chapter. There are hundreds of thousands of *shakha* around India. And, as is common, Balakrishnan was attracted because he liked the games they played. In Himmatnagar the game was called *kabbadi*. It is a curious proposition. There are two teams, and a player from one runs to the other, touching as many members as possible while shouting "*kabbadi, kabbadi, kabbadi*" over and over. If he stops shouting or he is caught, he's out.

"It builds teamwork and courage," Balakrishnan explained. "Then you learn self-improvement. I began to see that I could develop my personality in the RSS."

All this is common: Attract young people with games, build the ideology, the propaganda, and the proselytizing into the games, focus on the transformation of the self and, always, on the habits of inclusion and exclusion.

Night had fallen, and I had had enough of Balakrishnan. He had confirmed much but taught me little—apart from the rules of *kabbadi*.

When I made to leave, Balakrishnan said he wanted to mention one more thing.

"Of course," I replied.

"I believe in the RSS, but you know my best friend is Muslim. He's in the training service here."

AN INDIAN MOSAIC acquires many tiles over time. I have described a very few. But with his extraordinary remark about his friend, a piece of information I was to know so as to know him, Balakrishnan seemed in some fashion to put in place an important part of the mosaic I began many years ago but cannot hope to complete. Amid all the darkness, amid the forgetting and remembering and "remembering" in quotation marks, a flicker of light.

Readings

Chatterjee, Partha. *Nationalist Thought in the Colonial World.* Minneapolis, 1986.

———. *The Nation and Its Fragments.* Princeton, NJ, 1993.

Ci Jiwei. "The Confucian Relational Concept of the Person and Its Modern Predicament." *Kennedy Institute of Ethics Journal* 9, no. 4 (1999).

Connerton, Paul. *How Societies Remember.* Cambridge, UK, 1989.

Gupta, Dipankar. *Learning to Forget.* New Delhi, 2005.

Halbwachs, Maurice. *On Collective Memory.* Chicago, 1992.

Isozaki Arata. *Japan-ness in Architecture.* Cambridge, MA, 2006.

Kamenka, Eugene, ed. *Nationalism.* Canberra, 1973.

Mitscherlich, Alexander, and Margarete Mitscherlich. *The Inability to Mourn.* New York, 1975.

Nandy, Ashis. *The Illegitimacy of Nationalism.* New Delhi, 1994.

Nietzsche, Friedrich. *Untimely Meditations.* Cambridge, UK, 1997.

Nora, Pierre. "Between Memory and History: Les Lieux de Mémoire." *Representations* 26 (Spring 1989).

Parkes, Graham, ed. *Nietzsche and Asian Thought.* Chicago, 1991.

Ricoeur, Paul. *Memory, History, Forgetting.* Chicago, 2004.

Tagore, Rabindranath. *Nationalism.* Calcutta, 1996.

Watsuji Tetsuro. *Ancient Japanese Civilization.* Tokyo, 1920.

Yates, Frances A. *The Art of Memory.* Chicago, 1966.

The Skyward Garden

The essential thing is to overcome our inner void.
—KEIJI NISHITANI (1967)

1

L ET US RETURN to the place where we began, to the city that once took pride in its "smoke of seven colors." We must look once again at Kitakyushu. It is a city of one million people that is reinventing itself, imagining itself anew. And it is in such a reimagining that we find an answer to the question these essays pose: If the nineteenth century belonged to the West, and if we count the twentieth as one of transition, why shall we now consider the twenty-first someone else's?

To know Kitakyushu's past is to recognize its astonishing transformation in fewer than forty years. In the warm months children swim off the beaches that now line Dokai Bay. Restaurants serve fish from the harbor—a hundred varieties of it by the local count. Dozens of river walks, green zones, environmental museums, and ecological research facilities are spread across the city. And then the recycling plants: One recycles pinball machines, another printer cartridges; there is one for cars, one for home appliances, one for office equipment, one for fluorescent bulbs. It is a long list. *Mottai-nai,* "the shame of wastage," is the thought. It is not a new idea: It is a very old one, the idea of rice cultivators.

Kitakyushu issued the first smog alert in its history in 1969. It now proposes to make itself "the world capital of sustainable development," and there is nothing to suggest it cannot succeed. It has already earned world recognition as an "eco-city." Japan's first zero-emissions industrial zone operates along the waterfront. There are "ecological apartments," an "Eco Life" shopping mall selling products made of recycled materials, and hundreds of other such projects. The goal is shared—by residents, the corporations, the municipality—and it is simply stated in the city's abundant literature: "to realize the city in nature and nature in the city."

Now we can ask: What has happened in Kitakyushu? What momentous turn has occurred there? Why does it now embrace the ethos we know as green with a vigor that can remind us only of its former dedication to destroying itself? From our utilitarian point of view, we would conclude that the cost of the smoke of seven colors came to outweigh the benefits. This would be right but not enough, for as a summation of Kitakyushu's journey from the twentieth century to the twenty-first it deprives us of more understanding than it gives.

At city hall I met a man named Hiro Mizoguchi. We spoke in his office, with a row of wind turbines turning on a spotlessly blue horizon outside his window. He seemed an average bureaucrat: middle-aged, receding hairline, quietly dressed, and quietly going about his work. And perhaps he was average as an official in a city so given over to greenness. But our conversation turned out to be other than average. Mizoguchi was in charge of international cooperation in the city's environment department, and he had a sophisticated explanation of what had happened to Kitakyushu on its journey from an obsession with progress to an obsession with accommodation between man and technology and the natural world.

Mizoguchi began by telling me about certain words. One was *kankyo*, the Japanese for "environment." The first character, *kan*, signifies the relatedness of things; *kyo* means simply "one's world." *Kankyo*, environment: the connectedness of all things in the world we live in. Another term was *kyosei*, which has become a prevalent idea among the Japanese over the past decade or so. It means a symbiosis among diverse things, as against "dominance and monoculture," as Mizoguchi put it. There were other such words he was eager to explain. And I soon found myself in a philosophical exchange concerning science and the limits of science and the difference between Eastern and Western notions of humanity's place in nature. "We are subjects, a tree is an object," Mizoguchi offered. "But it is the tree that makes us subjects." And so on. It was not the sort of thing one expects to enter upon at any given city hall.

As we concluded our morning together, Mizoguchi made a remark that has stayed with me ever since. "We had our ideals and beliefs, but we decided to follow the West," he said. "We wanted progress in the Western way, so we forgot our own ways of thinking. Then, after a time, a certain impatience began to arise within us. And then our original beliefs came back."

WESTERNERS ARE OFTEN impatient with the kind of conversation I had with Hiro Mizoguchi. It is common to dismiss such exchanges as a sort of Eastern mystification of plain facts—in this case, a dirty city cleaned itself up. This is understandable. We Westerners are empiricists. What has been said of the Japanese and the Chinese in the nineteenth century is no more than our reflection in a mirror: We are interested primarily in what we can see. Sight is the sense we honor more than any other.

But we must look at Kiakyushu more fulsomely, with a more open eye. When we do, we find some interesting things. We find a unity of spirit and things that we have not found before, as if the city has at last grasped Gandhi's old thought: In the things we do and make do, we recognize our true reflections. We also find a new idea of "progress," one that takes a step beyond the West's. All over Asia we find addiction to the Western inheritance. But we cannot be satisfied simply with what seems everywhere the case. We have to look two other places at once if we are truly to understand: at the front edge of the Asian story and beneath its surface. And it is there beyond the manifest present that we discover, here and there, suggestions of things to come, aspirations beyond what meets the eye. The

East has made itself the world's industrial suburb, a friend in Beijing said not long ago. True enough, but we can hardly conclude that the story ends there.

This is Kitakyushu's lesson. It is exemplary of Asia's strongest impulse in our time—the impulse to discover itself again after a century and a half of lostness. This will mean many things. The separation of spirit and things, *ti* and *yong*, ends and means: This will at last disappear. Asia will understand itself as a place with a usable past but also (as we have used this term) as a place miscegenated, with background and foreground joined as one. In a word, the East will assume the habit of self-reference, with a self-generated idea of what it means to be modern. This is of immense importance, for it stands to make Asia a full partner in the present century rather than a taker of directions, a follower.

The change of consciousness Japan went through during the Meiji modernization was the most fundamental in the whole of its history. We see the same now, only it is occurring in reverse. Japan buried its past when it began to "follow the West," as Mizoguchi put it. We have used the term "museumization," but interment comes to the same thing. An essential connection was lost. The Japanese, and many others after them, lived no longer by their own trajectory but by someone else's. And now we find that they are unburying the past they once had lost and using it anew. They are doing nothing less than repossessing themselves. This is Asia today, here and there to one degree or another, and it is destined to alter this century.

This is not an exercise wherein the old traditions come out of musty museum displays and are found to be enchanting in an age short of traditions. That is the purview of conservative nationalists and cultural nostalgists—two kinds of people with oddly much in common. We are talking about quite the opposite. After a long history with the modern, a new tradition arises, a modern tradition. The sensation of having borrowed so much for so long gives way to an impulse to declare the validity of the imported and the right to choose it as one's own. We Westerners will never fully grasp the breakthrough this represents. But this is Asia's modern fate, to live with its miscegenated mix of the old and the once new and novel from somewhere else. "We can no longer tell the difference between what is 'Japanese' and what is 'Western,' " a friend in Tokyo once said. This is the point precisely.

I have engaged themes in these essays that I have come to view as fundamental to Asia's experience of the modern. Time, the self, nature: It seems an imposing list, but in each case the East has spent a century and a half absorbing a Western conception. Chronology was to be Western chronology. Past and present were to be reconceived as discontinuous, the one inaccessible to the other. The self was to be the ego-centered self, not the embedded self, the self within a larger community of one kind or another. Humanity was distinct from nature and acted upon it; it was not simply a constituent in the physical world. The primacy of science and the fragmentation of knowledge that the scientific perspective produces were accepted as inevitable parts of the modern. Always we find that the West brought an essential impulse to separate, one thing from another: past from present, individual from community, humanity from its earthly environment. The West brought segmentation, not continuity or conceptions of the whole. And this was taken to be what it meant to be modern.

Asia's struggle with these questions has been long and difficult, and it has resolved none completely. Instead, the East learned the art of doubling, or to live amid its own contradictions and ambiguities. But now we advance into a different kind of world, and each question is to be rethought. Time, the self, nature—redefinition in these matters, I believe, will be an essential feature of what I have come to call a post-Western era. "The shadows of the past are the promise of the future," Kakuzo Okakura wrote at the end of *The Ideals of the East*. This was prescient by a century, for we are now destined to reimagine our relations with all that lies behind us. We cannot pretend any longer to live so freely from the past. Neither can we any longer sustain our prevalent illusions—not too strong a term— as to the extreme autonomy of the individual. Neither will our planet much longer survive the West's presumption of humanity's mastery and infinite prerogative.

In certain ways this will invert the world as we customarily think of it. What were once Asia's great challenges and the West's great advantages in matters related to time, the individual, and nature are now to Asia's advantage and present themselves as challenges to the West. The same holds true in two other respects. Asia is accustomed to what I have called miscegenation; it is for the West to get used to it now, for miscegenation is our destiny. Equally, Asia has been ever restive with the nation-state—the West's most profound imposition in the nineteenth century. Now, in the twenty-first, there are already signs that Asians are prepared to look anew at this not-very-eternal idea, and in this, too, they are ahead of the West where they were once behind.

The process I describe is familiar by way of a term Nietzsche gave us. He called it revaluation, and he meant "the revaluation of values." Of what value are our values? This was the question urged upon us by the thinker who announced the modern condition before it had arrived. It is not an easy question, for to pose it we must accept that our values are provisional— contingent. Is science, for instance, so unassailably sufficient as we suppose as a path to knowledge and understanding? It is difficult, yes, but to ask the value of our values is the way to true renewal. It is the question vigorous societies put to themselves, Nietzsche suggested. And it is the question we find posed across Asia today. Let us recover our old, submerged ties with the past and with the natural world and find their worth again in our twenty-first-century lives and by way of our twenty-first-century technologies. Let us salvage something of the old belonging and combine it with something of the new. This is Kitakyushu's particular project. We find variations on the theme all over the East. One way or another they all entail a recovery of the self. This is what we mean by revaluation.

An endeavor of this kind lends a civilization an immense new strength—a durability, a way into the future, as Nietzsche understood. Here we must distinguish between strong nations and the merely powerful. It is because Asia has entered upon a process of revaluation that it stands to find again a strength it has not known for some centuries. So can we contemplate a post-Western world. This is a world, in its simplest definition, that thinks and lives beyond the frameworks to which we are accustomed—nineteenth-century frameworks, for the most part, ways of thinking and living we must, like it or not, outgrow.

I have never forgotten a certain habit of speech among the people of Calicut along the Malabar Coast. They commonly talk of "the da Gama epoch." The phrase is attractive for its suggestive power. It implies that the era of the West's superiority, which we customarily consider to be without end, turns out to have a beginning, a middle, and a conclusion. All epochs do, by definition, and we stand now at the far end of one: If we did not, we would lack perspective, and it would be impossible to talk in Calicut of an epoch begun by a Portuguese sailor five centuries ago.

FOR A LONG TIME we have understood the modern condition as involving a decisive and altogether desirable break with the past. This is what the West conveyed to the East in the nineteenth century, and it is what the West believed. The past is a prison, a heavy weight, and tradition no more than fetters, confinements. One could not be modern without accepting these as self-evident truths. Speed, altitude, machinery: These captivated the early moderns. They seemed to make humanity newly free. Artists were especially articulate on the point. Demolish museums and libraries, the Italian Futurists declared in their manifesto, published in 1909. A roaring car is more beautiful than the white marble of *Winged Victory,* a useless souvenir—a relic, as was the Louvre, where the famous Greek figure still resides. This was life-without-history as a glorious outcome.

How should primitive nations make themselves modern? This was a much-posed question in the 1950s and 1960s, as the world was required to define itself more emphatically than ever according to "East" and "West." The Western answer was simple: Backward people become modern people by following the example of the Europeans and the Americans, who had, after all, invented the very idea of progress. Progress was an emanation, originating "here" and spreading outward to "there"—from "us" to the "other." To modernize, then, meant to Westernize, and for others this meant to leave one's own past behind. In the academy this became known as modernization theory. All that was "primitive" or "traditional"—history itself— was cast in a new light and would be of little use.

The Japanese were the first non-Western people to sign on to this line of thinking. But this idea of the modern reached its zenith, fair to say, during the Cold War years. It was as powerful as any warhead, for it was made a matter of ideology. Nothing about one's identity or one's past counted so much as whether one were with the West or that darkened place known as the East.

It will be many years before we come fully to terms with the Cold War's consequences. But one is already apparent. A new idea of what it means to be modern has emerged since Germans dismantled the Berlin Wall in 1989. It became evident with startling speed afterward, as if it were a pent-up impulse— as, indeed, history will show it to have been. We saw, from early in the 1990s, an almost complete reversal of field. In one nation after another the old apposition between the traditional and the modern was dropped. Many questions still surround the past: What shall be kept from it, what modified, what discarded? But an authentic connection with one's history is now recognized as essential to becoming truly modern. The consequences reach far. What do we now mean by progress? In which direction does it lie, forward or back from where we stand? What about Tagore's thought a century ago that science must be properly applied? What do we think he meant by that? At the very least we must recognize that two centuries or more of Western thinking have been upended. To be modern no longer means to Westernize at the cost of one's past. This, too, is what we mean when we speak of a post-Western world.

It is not one in which roles are simplistically reversed, we must quickly add. True enough, we witness an accumulation of power in Asia and a relative decline in the influence of the West. This is almost certainly irreversible. When Western governments depend for their financial lifeblood on the Chinese and the Japanese, when Western companies go to the East in search of capital, when Asians assume leadership in diplomatic conflicts the West has found insoluble—at this point, plainly enough, we are living in something beyond the era of Western primacy. But to fret about an assertive Asia is to assume a nineteenth-century notion of power, and nineteenth-century thinking is the very mold that is breaking. What we can anticipate, conversely, is a historic redefining of the "imaginary line that separates East from West." Encounters across it will be among the essential experiences of our time, and influences are destined to flow in both directions.

Among the interesting philosophers of the twentieth century, in any culture or language, was a Japanese named Keiji Nishitani. He was part of what was known decades ago as the Kyoto school, a group much taken up with Japan's singular place in the modern world. Nishitani was a meticulous student of Nietzsche and, like the famous German, was often maligned by those who misappropriated his thinking, particularly his ideas as to the use of history and tradition.

In an essay published in his later years, Nishitani contemplated Japan's fate in a fashion as striking for its prescience as Okakura's thought on the past. It reflects the perspective that is ours at the end of one era and the start of another. It is an early intimation of the world we can now conceive of as post-Western, and what Nishitani says about Japan may be taken to apply to much of Asia:

> We Japanese have fallen heir to two completely different cultures . . . This is a great privilege that Westerners do not share in . . . but at the same time it puts a heavy responsibility on our shoulders: to lay the foundations of thought for a world in the making, for a new world united beyond differences of East and West.

IN TOKYO I HAD a long friendship with a man named Koichi Kato. Kato was a prominent member of the Diet and had been influential for many years in the long-governing Liberal Democratic Party. He had traveled extensively, and, as travel always does, it had given him a second pair of eyes. Kato saw Japan as a Japanese but also as others saw it.

The last time I met Kato, he was about to turn seventy and had been nearly forty years in the legislature. How far had Japan come? he wondered. Where was it headed next? He worried, in so many words, about the emptiness of Japanese affluence. Without using the term, he talked about the nihilism evident among the Japanese. The nation had wandered, he said, since the early 1990s—almost twenty years at the time of our conversation. There seemed to be no national aspiration, no purpose. America had such a purpose, the French believed in France, China had still to complete the project of making itself modern. But Japan had nothing to do or to say for itself. This was Kato's thinking.

"What will be our next goal?" he asked. "It's the first question for any country, and we've found no answer. We've caught up with the West only to discover we're a nation with no character."

Kato and I met, most of the time, in his messy, overstuffed office at the Diet. Out the window behind him was always the geometry of the Tokyo skyline—rows of tall, efficient towers, all in the austere International Style the Japanese favored during the postwar years of rebuilding. Often enough, a crane would be swiveling somewhere on the horizon. I had come to associate the backdrop with our exchanges.

Kato began to speculate during that last conversation.

"Maybe we can be a leader on environmental questions," he said. " 'Japan: the country with the greatest respect for nature.' Maybe this is our essence. Maybe we are meant to be mediators. 'Japan: a country between East and West.' "

Kato paused and gazed at the ceiling, exhaling a little wearily.

"Okay," he said, "respect for nature, a mediating nation. But how do you project these things? A mediator can't take pride in itself. And we want to be proud of our character, our essence, and ourselves."

Kato's thinking remains prevalent among the Japanese. "Power without purpose" has been a common critique of Japan for many years, and for many Japanese the thought has a sting to it. The 1990s are known as Japan's lost decade—years when it lost its economic vitality and drifted with no apparent aim, no place in the wider world. On the face of it, these criticisms seem self-evident. Japan still appears to drift, fair to say. Its only intent seems to be to preserve its comforts and security, and this seems acceptable to few as a national purpose.

"Why do nations need a purpose?" a particularly provocative

friend in Tokyo once asked me. "Of what purpose is a national purpose?"

Over some years I have found these to be among the most useful questions any Asian has ever posed in reply to a Westerner's inquiries. Had I not inherited the notion of national purpose and assumed its self-evident sense? In time, these questions gave me the key to why we must finally reject all notions of Japan as a wandering nation, a selfish nation, a nation with no aspirations. Instead, we must understand it as an emergent post-Western nation and recognize the difficulty of articulating this position—the heavy responsibility Keiji Nishitani felt settling on Japan's shoulders.

Where does the notion of national purpose come from? Where did we get this idea? Why do we find it admirable if a nation leads others? Why do we think nations should be powerful? Why do we assume that great nations are possessed of military might? Why should a nation be ever ready to assert itself? Why is a nation weak if it cannot do this? Why is national sovereignty a more or less inviolable principle to us? We must be tough-minded as we pose such questions. There is no place for *angélisme*, as the French call it. Unsullied idealism will not serve us if we are to get to the bottom of these matters. And idealist it would be to dismiss these questions.

The answers to all of them lie all in the same place. These values are from the nineteenth century, and they come from the West. They reflect a notion of the nation-state Westerners elaborated 150 years ago and then proceeded to export around the world. The experiment was a success, plainly— setting aside our many "failed states." We now live on a planet made of roughly 190 nations. A post-Western world, as we should begin to think of it, will not require us to erase the boundaries we have drawn around the globe. They are likely to remain—if not, indeed, multiply—for a long time. But we are required to reconsider all our assumptions about nations and what they are supposed to do. This is the starting point of our revaluation.

Many Westerners, and many others for that matter, may find it difficult to grasp the thought that a nation should be anything other than purposeful and powerful. It strikes too deeply into our most fundamental assumptions about ourselves and the meaning we read into our existence. But we must try. And we can begin by recognizing that Asia's ideas about nations will reflect Asia's cultural values just as the West's ideas are rooted in Western cultural values. So we must go back to what Masao Maruyama, one of Japan's great postwar thinkers, called the *basso ostinato* of the Japanese—the things that were submerged but never fully disappeared. And we find among them those values reflected in the Asian conception of humanity's place on our planet, values with a distinctly Buddhist imprint: "the active practice of inaction," "the purposeful doing of not doing." The thought is not Japan's alone. Neither is there anything exotic about it, for it is deeply rooted in Eastern culture. "Do that which consists of doing nothing," Laozi, the Chinese sage, counseled in (we think) the sixth century B.C.

It leads us to a certain paradox, probably the most formidable noted in these essays. We will be perplexed by it, as Koichi Kato and many other Japanese are themselves perplexed, for it requires the giving up of many thoughts. But it is among the essential features of our post-Western era, and so we must attempt it: It is the purpose of having no purpose. It reflects, at bottom, a different idea of power and how it is exercised, of what it means to be a nation. As a start, we may consider where our past century or so of great national purpose has landed us. It is difficult to admire the record.

Americans, in particular, will stumble on the thought. Americans think of great nations as powerful, assertive, and individual in the way they act among others because these are among the values Americans hold high. A nation cannot be a nation

without a purpose. This is why Americans have never suc-
ceeded in living for long without an enemy. Enemies, even if
they are half-imagined, give purpose. And we are now con-
fronted with an epoch in which it is proposed that having no
national purpose, at least as we have come to think of it, is a
nation's purpose. It will be long before we are able to accommodate this, and perhaps we will never manage it. It seems, on
the face of it, to rank among the perversities of our time. But
sooner or later we will have to bid farewell to missions, civilizing or otherwise, for missions as we have long understood them
are of another time.

We have, indeed, already begun to devise terms to make
this notion less strange. When we speak of "soft power," we
mean leadership without leading: to lead not assertively, in
nineteenth-century fashion, but as a model—actively leaving
assertion out of it. Think again of Kitakyushu: This is the very
essence of the project. We believe it is possible to live better
lives by combining all our advanced technology with a deep
and ancient respect for nature, and we will lead the way simply
by doing so: This is the message Kitakyushu has for us.

Equally, there is the prospect of multipolarity, which I view
as inevitable however much or long Americans may resist it.
The term gives a more palatable way to dispose of outdated
ideas. It is quintessentially post-Western, whether or not we
recognize it as such. A multipolar world is one in which everyone leads together or there are no leaders as we traditionally
think of them. We can put it either way, but the point remains:
We are destined to revalue leadership in the post-Western era,
just as we are challenged to revalue mission and purpose.

THIS IS THE FIRST TIME an Asian nation has come to advance its
own idea of what a nation should be. From the Meiji Restoration until now, Japan has lived according to the West's idea.
The Pacific war, for instance: It can be cast as an attempt to
emulate Western-style national assertion. Then the postwar

period of apparent passivity: a refusal to act any longer in the Western manner, a subtle act of resistance. This perspective reveals many things. Most important, Japan's thinking will differ from the West's because it is reaching back into its own tradition. Strange it would be if Japan's idea of what a nation should be turned out to be perfectly congruent with ours in the West.

There is much worth considering in this light. We can understand anew the commitment most Japanese have to pacifism, for instance. The pacifist principle was given to the Japanese in the constitution Americans wrote and required them to adopt in 1947. It is contained in Article 9, and the passage has been a point of contention ever since. Nationalists oppose it as an imposed doctrine that makes Japan other than a "normal nation," while the majority of Japanese strongly favor it. This debate has sharpened in recent years. It is fundamentally about two different conceptions of the nation. Conservatives and ultranationalists hold to the nineteenth-century view. When they say Japan must become a normal nation, they mean it as this was meant a century and more ago. From their perspective Japan did during the war only what it learned from its Western adversaries. Those favoring the "peace constitution" take a twenty-first-century view—a post-Western view. From this perspective, Japan's error in the Pacific war was one of self-betrayal—it had acted against its own deepest principles. I have thought for many years that Japan should debate the 1947 constitution and write a new one of its own. It is almost certain, however, that any such document would incorporate either the pacifist Article 9 or a clause very like it.

Let us consider the so-called lost decade from the same point of view. We find, not so oddly, that it was nothing like lost. That we consider it so reflects nothing more than our utilitarian thinking. We saw nothing of the whole—a measure of how inadequate our habits of mind have become.

Japan was a great disappointment for many people in the 1990s. Having watched it amass immense wealth, we wondered how it would manifest its new global influence. Would the yen become a reserve currency, competing with the dollar? Would Japan assert itself in institutions such as the World Bank? Would it articulate a new voice in international conflicts? Not much of this came to be. Instead, Japan fell into a prolonged malaise and never seemed to grasp the leadership role opened to it—not in Asia, not anywhere else. Some native diffidence, or at worst indifference, appeared to prevail. "Lost," most of us said, and many Japanese seemed to agree.

I have never accepted this thesis. Something else has been occurring, something easy to miss. But if one looks closely, it becomes easier to recognize that Japan was starting a vast new project—a revaluation involving two Japans: Japan as it had been buried and the modern Japan that did the burying. How shall we live in Japan as it is? the Japanese began to ask. Japan spent the 1990s formulating this question. There is nothing lost or wasteful in such an undertaking. What it now stutters to articulate will be old and new and non-Western all at once. And the way it articulates itself will also be other than the Western way. This gives us a more accurate accounting of Japan since the 1990s than any theme of lostness. The "lost decade" thesis was always too simplistic, an unseeing outsider's idea, a utilitarian's idea. "Power without purpose" was rooted in outdated assumptions. It is nineteenth century—a misinterpretation. "Power without projection" is the accurate rendering. To put the point simply about the Japanese, they only looked lost.

The project I describe does not sit plainly on the surface of life, although it is apparent enough in places such as Kitakyushu. It will not give Japan steel plants and shipyards, as Meiji did, but most Japanese who are articulate on the topic liken it to the Meiji years. They mean this in two ways: It will match Meiji in its historical importance, and it will take about as long. Meiji altered Japan's course forever; so will its emergence as Asia's first post-Western nation. Meiji lasted roughly forty years; if history gives us any symmetry, which is unpredictable,

Japan is about halfway through its revaluation of itself and its place in the world.

What will Japan look like in another twenty years? How will it act?

These questions are pertinent to much of Asia, for much of Asia seems once again set to follow the Japanese as it did in the nineteenth century. This makes them especially good questions. The answers bring us to the core of the matter as we have already considered it. Time, self, nature: It is Japan's thoughts on these things that will tell us what kind of nation it will be.

ONE AUGUST EVENING in Tokyo, I met a man named Senjaku Nakamura. He was known all over Japan as Senjaku, his given name, because he came from many generations of actors and was among the country's most celebrated Kabuki players. We were seated side by side at what turned out to be a curious gathering. It was hosted by a prominent chief executive and was à la mode in every way: flowing champagne, a string quartet, beautiful table linens, beautiful food. Yet the occasion took place in a house meticulously restored in village Japanese style—a simple house of wood and tatami, elegant in a different way. Outside the dining room was a garden worthy of a Zen monastery.

Senjaku and I spent the evening talking. How did an actor dedicated to a great tradition take in such an eclectic scene? What did it mean to perform Kabuki in the twenty-first century? The setting seemed to put the questions squarely between us. Eventually we agreed to meet. A new season was just beginning at Kabuki-za, the famous theater in the Ginza district. I was to go to Senjaku's dressing room between performances.

Senjaku greeted me in his underwear, still perspiring from the performance he had just finished—a dance based on an old Noh drama. We sat on tatami while he scrubbed off his makeup and watched a baseball game. He kept the game on as we conversed, and I sensed it was part of the point he was eager to make.

"When you watch later," he said, "remember what we're thinking onstage. What's important is not the continuing of a great art with a long past but what we must do now to please those who come to see us. Kabuki is more than a collection of museum pieces."

The program that day was as interesting as Senjaku promised. There was the dance taken from Noh, then a one-act first performed in 1746, then a satire written for Kabuki in the 1920s, and then a new Japanese version of Verdi's *Aïda*. But the best piece was one from the 1970s called *Yasunosuka's Search for a Home*. It concerned a young boy's reunion with his mother after many years apart—an interesting premise in itself. It was full of the conflicts and emotions familiar to anyone now living—modern conflicts, modern emotions—but it took place in the Tenpo era, the 1830s, an anticipatory interlude just before the Meiji modernizations began, and it was acted in period costume.

Senjaku and Kabuki-*za* suggested something essential about the Japan that is gradually emerging. Japan can often seem fated to live in an eternal state of looking back. Reflecting its peculiar path into the modern, it appears always to portray itself to itself as Senjaku did in the play set 180 years earlier—by way of the past, the past that was before the burying began. One finds this everywhere. The man who introduced Senjaku and me, the host at dinner, was the most up-to-date of executives. And, eccentrically enough, he kept a small rice terrace in the basement of his corporate headquarters in central Tokyo. You stepped off the elevator to the reek of mulch and fertilizer and the glare of high-technology lighting. "Our values are village values," this curious man said when asked to explain. "To me this is a wonderful dream. It is Japan as we've made it."

Lafcadio Hearn warned of this a hundred years ago. Amid all the modernizing, Japan will come to regret all it had given up, he wrote at the turn of the last century. Again, it seems prescient. But we see now a determination to advance beyond the

cul-de-sac of regret and nostalgia. It is leading Japan to seek a
synthesis of the old and the new that is a third thing, altogether
new in our world. The boundaries the West draws across
time—this is the present, there is the past—are being erased.

It is useful to think of this as the final phase of the Meiji project, for it also involves that most unresolved of Japan's modern
questions—the question of the self, how to belong. This is the
issue Japan is poised to settle—the problem of *shutai-sei*, as they
put it in the 1950s, individual autonomy. Time has tumbled a
half century forward now. The old debates and the desire for
greater individuality were based on Western concepts of subjectivity. This is why they never fully took hold. What we must
look for now is a synthesis, another instance of miscegenation.
The old idea of belonging is not to be discarded but kept and
reimagined. We can return again to the notions of assurance
and trust: The one describes a society based on village familiarity, the other one of strangers dependent on the social compact
we broadly think of as trust. The synthesis will consist of both.

We can already detect a certain evolution, particularly since
the Liberal Democrats, who had governed for most of the postwar era, were turned out of office in 2009—a watershed election. It is evident that the emerging Japan is destined to
resemble the social democracies of Europe far more than it will
America, despite living under the latter's tutelage for the past
sixty years. Once Japan completes its long-running economic
reforms, we will discover it to have built a "social market" system more or less on the lines of Germany's. Its political system,
after nearly a century of struggle with the political equation, is
already beginning to look like Continental Europe's, not America's. Its corporations have developed a hybrid management
model: Western methods in finance and technology, symbiotic
relations between company and community and company and
employee. The Japanese company, as far back as the seventeenth century (when the first of them, Mitsui, was founded),
has always been considered an *ie*, an extended household. In the

post-Western era this notion is to be preserved in twenty-first-century form.

THERE IS A BUILDING in Tokyo's central business district that I see whenever I am in Japan. One gets a full view of it from the library at the Foreign Correspondents' Club, which occupies a high floor in a neighboring office block. I have spent some hours over many years staring at the odd edifice across the way. I keep a few photographs of it in a notebook, for it bears an essential lesson.

From the street it appears to be a commercial building like any other: plate-glass retail space on the ground floor, stories of identical windows above with identically placed office lighting in each. Above the street you see something else. At the tenth story or so the architect designed an immense hole into the structure. In it you find a well-kept Japanese garden: trained pines, perfectly trimmed shrubs, gravel walks, rocks placed meticulously here and there.

Let us not be falsely kind. As architecture the thing comes to us as an oddity, a one-off in no need of repeating. But as a statement of aspiration this building is eloquent. It is an embrace of the miscegenated present, a refusal to object any longer to Japan as it is.

I was walking by it one day a few summers ago with a young friend. I told him about it, and crossing the street and craning his neck, he could make out the edges of the skyward garden. Then my friend began telling me about *jinbei*. *Jinbei* go back to premodern Japan. They are the loose cotton clothing still worn at summer festivals or during weekends around the house. "You feel more natural," my friend said when he explained the change that came over him when he changed his clothes. "It's a question of *wa*, harmony. You're more in tune with who you are. You're more Japanese."

At first I could not follow my friend's thread. Why did he

think of *jinbei* after seeing the garden? Then it came to me. The old clothing and the garden built into an office tower were remnants of the same thing, the old impulse toward doubling. But there was no doubling now; there was a oneness in these gestures, an acceptance of Japan as it has become—as it is. The impulse and the feeling will always remain. But there was nothing of lostness or regret or resistance left in either as I saw them then, for there is nothing, at last, that has been lost or requires regret. There is nothing to resist. In place of the void comes a certain fullness, self-possession in its truest meaning.

THE MOST CAPTIVATING PLACE in all of China, if I had to choose one, lies half-hidden in Suzhou, the old center of silk and prosperous merchants along the lower reaches of the Yangtze near Shanghai. It sits in a corner of the city's most famous sight, a Ming creation called the Humble Administrator's Garden. Here we find a text, a narrative of China in the modern era.

You enter the Hall of Thirty-six Pairs of Mandarin Ducks by way of what remains of a Ming bridge. Things change once within the hall, however, for the Qing did much tampering at this end of the garden in the nineteenth century, just as they were considering the *li* and *yong* of China and the arriving West. The hall was a place of repose, where one gazed out at floating lotus flowers and the ducks that gave the place its name. Its rooms remain intact, filled with calligraphy, porcelain, and other treasures of the tradition. But the Qing replaced the walls, oddly, with panels of stained glass, speckled with medallions of brilliant blue.

"Original," my guide pointed out.

"They're Chinese, the glass panels?"

"Original imports from France, in the 1860s."

You exit the hall across another bridge, and this, too, was among the late Qing's renovations. Instead of stone, it is made of ornamental wrought iron, that material so expressive of Europe's industrial age. Instead of Ming eaves, grapevines hang from the ironwork. The characters for "good health, long life" are woven into the design. It looks like something Monet, in a chinoiserie phase, could have put in his famous gardens at Giverny: The French master might have imagined China as well as China imagined the nineteenth-century West.

Gardens are narratives in the Chinese tradition. A landscape is intended to present an illusion of the wider world by way of constructed scenes. And so you stand on the far side of the wrought-iron bridge, turn back, and gaze at the hall and its approaches and its stained glass. It makes, altogether, a strange sight and an interesting story. It begins as Chinese, through the middle it is Chinese and Western, and it ends with an object wholly Western but for its decorative elaborations.

The Hall of Ducks is China's modern story. It seems to sit entirely unconscious of the tale it tells. But it is an exquisite expression of China as it is. It is why we must compare China today with the Japan of the 1880s, not the 1980s, for China is still preoccupied, if not voraciously obsessed, with the acquisition of Western things.

I COMPLETED THESE ESSAYS in the autumn of 2009, a few months after the twentieth anniversary of the Tian'anmen Square incident. It was a bitter moment, not only because Tian'anmen has been so thoroughly erased in China's memory, but also because of what had come to China since 1989—what had come instead of the dream of another, different future. Things are important to the Chinese. We cannot diminish the priority given to material well-being in what amounts to a culture of poverty. But with things alone comes what we recognize as consumerist nihilism, and China is awash in it. Tian'anmen went unmarked on the mainland, but the bittersweet smile can be counted its marker. The truth of what I had learned in India was China's truth: The moment of "success" becomes the moment of defeat. History's trick still repeats itself.

Asia is not altogether one as it enters the post-Western era. The subtle shift toward wholeness and self-possession one finds among the Japanese is not yet evident across the East China Sea, or is evident only here and there. China, like Japan a century ago, is still trying to prove that technological modernization is culturally unimportant—the one, supposedly, has nothing to do with the other. The Chinese state is the show master in this respect. And so come certain realities. We must recognize the limited extent to which the Communist Party, in any of its phases, has brought a break with the past. It is now nearly a century since the collapse of the Qing, but what should succeed the Qing has yet to be settled. China seems not to manage without an emperor or an equivalent, and it cannot "become modern" so long as it has one.

The Chinese live today according to a certain social contract. It is undeclared anywhere, but every Chinese knows the terms. It involves a fundamental exchange between those in power and those without it. Those with power are to go unchallenged. In return, those without it are permitted to prosper. To put it another way, politics is to be left to the bureaucratic elite and the party; commerce and the economy are the confines of the citizenry. Democracy is forgone, but the deprivation is assuaged by a considerable measure of material plenty.

There are features of the contract that those favoring it can be relied upon to emphasize. It produces high rates of growth. It also allows a certain kind of freedom. It is often asserted, indeed, that China is effectively freer than many democratic countries, and this is true so long as one understands the limits of this freedom. If you want to be corrupt in business or bend this or that rule or regulation, you are more or less free to try, but the agreement is plain: Do what you like within the fixed frame, but do not approach the borders of the frame.

The problems this social contract produces are equally plain.
It has always proven brittle, especially during recessions. When
prosperity ebbs, the system breaks down. This kind of social
contract also produces what we can call (borrowing a phrase
from an Indian thinker) "governmental technologies." Se-
questered bureaucracies of this kind draw their legitimacy only
nominally from their popularity, or even from the reluctant
acceptance of the citizenry. Their true justification is as providers
of services and efficiency. This partly reflects how the idea of a
nation came to Asia. It did not come as a choice made by those
who would live in it. The nation arrived as another machine,
and there is a consequent tendency to operate it as if it were a
machine.

We might just as well call China's social contract the Asian
social contract, for we have seen it many places beyond the
mainland. South Korea under its dictators, Indonesia under
Suharto, the Philippines under Marcos, Singapore under Lee
Kuan Yew (and his successors): All of these nations were allies
of the United States during the Cold War. And in all but Singapore, the social contract they enforced was dispensed with at
the Cold War's end. It casts China in an odd light. Why has it
chosen to put this contract in place at the very moment other
Asians have finished with it?

I posed this question for a long time. But it was not framed
correctly, I eventually concluded. The Asian social contract
first emerged in Meiji Japan, in the nineteenth century. It was
the method the Meiji oligarchs used to confine Japan's imports
from the West to material objects as against values. So it was
the way spirit and things, *ti* and *yong*, were separated. "Asian
values" is a term sometimes used to justify the Asian social contract, but "Asian values" are nothing more than a restatement
of the old spirit-and-things error. This is China today. Amid
what must be the most massive Westernization project in
human history, only technology and method are permitted to
enter. Life in such a condition becomes all *yong*, all material

objects. This produces the bittersweet smile—the smile and the nihilism that lies like a subterranean ocean beneath it. And this is why, if China is finally to succeed in its project of becoming modern, the social contract has to be broken.

How shall this be accomplished? Where in its own past will China rediscover itself, and so begin to reimagine its future?

ON THE LONG train journey from Hong Kong to Beijing, I once met a woman named Wang Yan. She was of late middle age, and she remains among the most enigmatic people I have ever known in China.

She had trained in chemistry and taught the subject for many years in the provinces. Then the reforms came, and Wang made herself an entrepreneur. She called this "diving into the ocean," meaning "entering the business world." She began with a travel agency. Some airplanes were acquired. And by the time I met Wang, there were so many businesses that her calling card doubled over so it could list them all. There was an advertising agency, an import-export firm, a high-technology company, an investment group, a company dealing in medical equipment. All of these were part of an empire called Sinoway.

When we reached Beijing, Wang and I agreed to meet, and over many weeks I came to know her story well—or as well as she would let it be known. Sinoway's offices turned out to be a large villa in a government compound ordinarily reserved for visiting dignitaries. And none of the businesses we had talked about on the train interested Wang so much as her latest. This was called Fairyland Health. It was a theme park on the outskirts of Beijing, and it was the first of its kind, Wang explained: a place where China's rich medical traditions and the wisdom of its ancient books were combined with a Western form—the inspiration being, of all things, Disneyland.

Wang said once, as we sat talking at a dining table in her villa, "My aim is to combine past and present, East and West.

This is the 'way' of Sinoway. We use modern science and modern forms to interpret China's great tradition so modern people can understand it. It's important for China in the twenty-first century to inherit the old, the wisdom of the ancestors."

Wang used to hold forth at length in this way. On other matters she was less forthcoming. She was investing more than 1 billion yuan, $130 million, in Fairyland Health—which turned out to be, indeed, a valuable tract of land in a section of the capital that was growing quickly. But I never learned how she had acquired those many acres, or where all the money came from, or why Sinoway had come to have offices in a state-owned villa. No one I knew in the financial markets had ever heard of Sinoway. After a time I began to guess that Wang had connections of some kind within the Communist Party. But I never learned. And when I shifted our conversation away from the *Yi' Jing* and Laozi and pressed Wang on these matters, our acquaintance quickly drew to a close.

Money and assets that come from no one knows quite where—this is a common story in China. What made me curious about Wang was her aspiration, however little or much of it she may ever realize. It was to bring something new into the world, to originate. It was to carry forward the past, however much the Chinese past had shifted and changed over the last century. It was, above all, to answer the West, to offer a reply. She understood that all the Westernization occurring around her was merely to imitate, in the modern Asian tradition. It kept China within the confines of the copyist.

I admired Wang for seeking an answer to this conundrum. But she was, in the end, no more than a nostalgist. She reminded me, during her long presentations, of all the Confucian revivalists I had met, perfecting their movements and wearing Han dynasty robes. This is not, once again, a usable past. To discover such a past requires the Chinese to step into what I called, at the start of these essays, the foreground of their history. And there we find rich soil. We find the decades between the collapse of the old order—the demise of the Qing in 1911—and Mao's rise to power in 1949. This describes a period of not quite forty years. It is the era of Xie Yong's "lost universities," the era Xie Tao, the old socialist in Chengdu, spoke of so movingly as one of diversity, exploration, and intellectual freedom. It seemed to suggest the promise that disorder sometimes holds. It was possible to be neither Eastern nor Western during this brief time, but rather both at once. For once, and briefly, the Chinese had gone beyond the phenomenon we call doubling; there was a unified self. And it is in this time that China can find the key to its contemporary destiny. China can again make itself what it was close to making itself then.

There is another way to put this, appropriate to the moment. Mr. Science and Mr. Democracy, those curious interwar figures, must finally learn to walk together. It will be a uniquely Chinese walk, but it will be a duet promenade. In a way of its own choosing, China must democratize: This is hardly an original thought. The worthwhile point is that China has a past, a modern tradition, from which to draw. We can cancel, then, any idea that democracy in China is an impossibility, a dream never to be realized. This is to misunderstand the Chinese and what they are capable of and the possibilities that lie in the foreground of their past. Tian'anmen was a politically immature event—this is now evident, however heroically we wish to cast it. Equally immature is any impulse to abandon the project, kicking the dirt and saying it cannot be done.

ON A VISIT TO BEIJING not long ago, just after a Lunar New Year had passed, I stayed with friends in the northwest corner of the capital. They lived in a new residential neighborhood, and like much else in urbanizing China—apartment towers, office towers, monorails, expressways, ring roads—it was a recent addition to a landscape that is being reinvented with that compulsive determination so characteristic of China in our time.

Late one afternoon my colleague during much travel over a long period came to visit. Zhuang Xi and I were planning an extensive journey to the southwest. Zhuang was the new China made flesh. She had been to Canada and returned with an advanced degree, perfected English, and before her a promising career made, if anything, of too many choices. I called her Shae, the Western name she had chosen.

As night fell, we waited outside for Shae's taxi to arrive. There were a hundred or so houses around us, all in the Western style: stout, three-storied dwellings with standard variations—a gabled roof, a Dutch Colonial, a Victorian turret, a Palladian window. We could have been in a suburb of Philadelphia. The only hints we were not were a few paper lanterns hung during the New Year and a pair of stone lions, lost at the end of a walk amid bicycles and green garbage bins.

These developments are common now in the big urban centers—Beijing, Shanghai, Guangzhou. They are the look of post-reform, ambitious-for-itself China. But Shae never seemed to have spent time in one. As her gaze wandered, her face seemed to fall a little, her composure flagged, and her animation deserted her.

"It's strange, isn't it?" she asked, dusk enveloping her words.

"The speed of it," I replied. "A couple of years ago this would've been fields, farmers' huts, and old stone walls."

"It's not that," Shae said. "There's no longer anything that's Chinese."

The moment and the observation have ever since held much for me. In Shae's chagrin, the makings of another bittersweet smile. In the wonder of her eyes, the waking from a dream.

. . .

IN KARNATAKA, a large, poor state in central India, I once encountered a man named Harsha Moily. He was in his thirties and came from a prominent Bangalore family. Moily had earned advanced degrees in America and had worked for some years on Wall Street and in the City of London. Then, a couple of years before we met, he had left behind his life as an NRI, a nonresident Indian, and gone home. Then he went to Bagalkot, among the poorest of Karnataka's twenty-eight districts, and began providing micro-finance to farmers and villagers.

"There was an election in 2004," Moily once explained. "The BJP"—the Bharatiya Janata Party, the Hindu nationalists—"had a campaign slogan. 'India is shining,' it said. I couldn't understand this. For 70 percent of the population India was not shining. So I watched closely. We used electronic voting machines across India for the first time, and rural India came out in the largest numbers in history to vote the BJP out."

Moily paused to reflect. Then: "That was a powerful moment for me. Poor villagers had said, 'Give us access and we'll take it.' They also said, 'We're comfortable with technology and we'll use it.' All this said to me, 'It's time to do something in the countryside.'"

Many things lay within Moily's story. One sometimes finds an impulse among NRIs now to return to the country they left in search of something better, for however much one achieves elsewhere, there is always the matter of identity—the pull of being Indian. Then the poor rural voters: They suggested much about heterogeneous time and what happens, the spark that ignites, when technology spreads into even the poorest parts of the country—when India finally shows up. There was also something in Moily's account about India's multiplicity, the many ways of belonging among Indians, and the kind of democracy India must invent to accommodate its multiple identities. And then the voting machines: I was curious and decided to look into them. They turned out to be purely of India's devising, made by a state-owned company—two hundred dollars each, the size of a suitcase, dust-proof and hack-proof.

Moily's account of his life and work among the poor in Karnataka eventually reminded me of a brief but poignant passage Nehru included in *The Discovery of India*. It concerned the matter of poise. To accept all that is modern, to be at home with it without losing oneself or one's connection to one's own past: This is poise, as I understand Nehru's meaning. India had had it once and lost it, Nehru said—a casualty of the modern era. Then he wrote:

> Is poise essentially static and opposed to progressive change? Must we sacrifice one for the other? Surely it should be possible to have a union of poise and inner and outer progress, of the wisdom of the old with the science and the vigor of the new. Indeed we appear to have arrived at a stage in the world's history when the only alternative to such a union is likely to be the destruction and undoing of both.

Nehru made these observations during a time he spent in a British jail, sixty years before the voters in Karnataka cast their electronic ballots. Did they not display precisely what Nehru was searching for—the poise that derives from certainty as to one's own past and a capacity to carry this forward into one's own time? This is India as it emerges into our post-Western century. It has regained some of its poise, perhaps we can say much, since Nehru wrote, a few years before independence. It seems, indeed, singularly gifted in this way. But it faces questions now. Will it remain so poised? Will India keep that aplomb history seems to have bequeathed so generously to it?

I KNEW AN ARTIST named S. Nandagopal, and I called him Nanda. He lived in an artists' colony on the sea near Madras, a famous place in India's artistic circles, and there he made "narrative sculptures," as he called them. They were welded works in copper and brass that combined themes and motifs from the ancient past—the past that lay all around him—with the formal advances of modern art. The effect was singular: a raw, primitive vitality expressed in a contemporary artistic vocabulary. "When I began, I had fifty years of modern Indian art before me," I remember Nanda saying one afternoon in his studio. "I couldn't ignore that. We once used to discuss 'Is it Indian or is it Western?' But that's the question of an earlier moment. I can't begin by saying 'I don't know my time.' "

There is an almost magical paradox in Nanda's work. His pieces are declaratively Indian and could be made nowhere else. Yet he has gone beyond all questions of "Indianness," of definition, of "East" and "West," of what is "ours" from the past and "theirs" from the modern era. There is a rich past in Nanda's art, but there is no nostalgia—"no looking back," as he once put it. And in this Nanda taught me the paradox buried in the thought of being post-Western. It is not to decide that the West is somehow to be ignored, countered, or is no longer of any use. It is to exit the frame, to step outside any thought of what is background or foreground or Western or Indian. This, surely, is also the poise of which Nehru wrote. And it is from this India can draw, if it so chooses, as it enters a new epoch.

Two great choices confront India. One concerns the nation's participation in the process of globalization. What shall the West be for India—influence, as it was for Nanda in his metalwork, or model? The choice comes late, if we consider India next to Japan or China. But this question of timing, the moment in history, affords India an opportunity. It can use its singular imagination to redefine globalism for all of us. By way of its eccentric tradition it can bring a critical sensibility to the globalization process, just as it has to the process of becoming modern. It can show us a fundamental truth: As there is not a single modernity, so is there no single form of globalization.

The latter is, properly understood, a two-way street, a hybrid wherever it appears, as against an emanation outward from the West. A global society need not be a mass society. The one, indeed, can replace the other. Difference is not to be "overcome" as something regrettable but embraced and transcended; a true individuality can replace the atomization so characteristic of the twentieth century. It was Ryszard Kapuściński, a truly twenty-first-century man, who urged these thoughts upon us at the very end of his many travels.

In all of this, nothing from East or West is to be cast aside— only all thought that one is to be privileged above the other. India, because of its past and what it now is, is better placed than most of us to take such a transforming role. Its problems are urgent and altogether Indian, not the West's. By definition it must find its own solutions, and from its example all of us can draw. The electronic voting machines: They are a small but evident case. Micro-finance, which has spread across India like a densely woven carpet, is another: One look at India suggests that it is a response to poverty that Indians are almost fated to develop more fully than anyone else.

India's other choice concerns its future as a secular democracy. If India is to survive as one, it will have to imagine itself anew. It will have to reinvent democracy and the nation, in effect, to make a democracy and a nation without a dominant culture. It cannot think of either secularism or democracy made valid because they have been tried and proven workable elsewhere. Secularism, in particular, cannot be made an article of faith as we have made it in the West. That is not progress, a true advance. Instead, India must think for itself and find an idea of the secular and the democratic that arises from the soil of its own past and reflects India as it is.

"In India everyone knows about religion," my young acquaintance from the RSS had said when we met and talked in Ahmedabad. What he meant, I was certain afterward, was better put this way: In India everyone knows through religion—

by way of it. India cannot surrender the value of freedom within a secular democracy even in the face of such a reality. Certainly it cannot give in to "political Hinduism" without suffering tragic consequences. But neither can it simply go on trying to import an off-the-shelf model of Western secularism, church and state as rigorously exclusive. It must, rather, invent a secularism that prevails by way of accommodation and coexistence even as it brims with religiosity. This, indeed, is closer to what George Holyoake, the English journalist and freethinker (and eccentric) meant when he gave us the term "secularism" in the mid-nineteenth century. This is also democracy without a dominant culture. In a society with many roots running deeply and diversely, it seems the only sustainable alternative.

These are India's choices. There are as yet no foregone conclusions to draw. Contemplating the violence in Gujarat a few years ago, a prominent Indian journalist wrote movingly about the country's trajectory, its self-doubt, and its fragility. "Is it possible that contrary to all the hoopla we may have already lived out the high tide of our democracy?" he asked. "Many Indians may get richer and richer but as a people—a deep civilization—we will now only get poorer and poorer? Is it possible that a country sprung from the vision of giants can now only sustain small men with small concerns?" This is India's trepidation as it enters the new century, as plainly stated as I have ever heard it or read of it.

"What is it we can bring to the table?" an executive in Hyderabad, a man named Ajit Rangnekar, once wondered aloud as we sat in his glass-box office. "Can we do something of our own? Will our anxieties make us look for alternatives?" The best one can say is that these questions, like those of the journalist looking back to the devastation in Gujarat, are posed all over India now. And if Indians choose wisely, they can transform themselves into genuine producers of the modern, as the Japanese seem likely to do.

Contemplating India's choices once, a scholar friend in

Ahmedabad made a memorable remark about both of them. We were talking about the prospects for preserving the eccentric tradition and the tremendous use to which India could put it.

"India owes this to itself," I said.

"India owes it to the world."

2

Look at the Other's face as he offers it to you. Through this face he shows you yourself.

—Ryszard Kapuściński, *The Viennese Lectures* (2004)

NOT LONG AGO, an Italian thinker named Franco Moretti advanced an interesting thesis on the history of the novel. We are accustomed to thinking of the modern novel as a Western form. When others took it up, they applied Western form and technique to local experience. So there was a dissonance: Western method, non-Western (Japanese, Chinese, Indian, and so on) substance.

Moretti had a different way to think about this. How many scores of thousands of novels have been written since the eighteenth century, and what small proportion, at this point, have been written by Westerners? The line of inquiry causes us to conclude that what we think of as the rule—Western technique applied to Western experience—has become the exception. The rule is now the inverse: Western form applied, with infinite variation, to non-Western experience. In the context of world literature, what we mean when we speak of the novel must be rethought more or less from top to bottom.

Moretti's thinking remains much debated, but we can borrow a little of it and bend it to a purpose, for it urges many questions upon us. What will we mean by democracy when most of the world accepts it as of universal value and we—we Westerners—are a small number of those living in democratic societies? There are not too many answers to this yet, but many await us. Democracy is destined to mean something different wherever it is adopted. If the West's own desires as to democracy's spread are fulfilled, we will live in a world wherein it is a matter of theme and incessant variation. It will prove, over and over, Western form and local application. We need look no further than India, or Japan today, to understand the point. In the latter's search for a new balance between trust and assurance, the strange and the village-familiar, it seeks nothing more than a kind of democracy that is its own.

From here the questions stretch out before us almost infinitely. What do we mean by the polity? What do we mean by the rights of the individual within it? What do we mean— an example already mentioned—by a secular society? What degree of freedom will be available in a free market? What is the place of the corporation in the community? Some of these matters are already upon us. What we call corporate social responsibility is a body of ideas informed by post-Western thinking. The economic crisis of 2008, fair to say, can be taken as an announcement that the question of managed markets will be settled only when post-Western ideas are taken into account. The Group of Seven, consisting of as many Western nations, has already given way to the Group of Eight, with Russia included. This now yields to the Group of Twenty, a mix of Western and non-Western nations. This is the post-Western world arriving.

"Enlightenment is man's release from his self-incurred tutelage," Kant wrote in 1784. "Tutelage is man's inability to make use of his understanding without direction from another." We may stumble on Kant's severity, for "self-incurred" does not seem altogether fair when we think of Asia's long age of tutelage. But his implications stand. To cast aside tutelage can lead only to open-ended outcomes. Those who achieve enlightenment, in Kant's conception, will by definition reach their own understanding of things. Strange the world would be if everyone's understanding of a given question were to match everyone else's.

The conclusion is evident. The West is no longer the master of the modern. The Enlightenment vision must be scrutinized and reimagined from a non-Western point of view, much as Franco Moretti looked again at the novel. The Atlantic world is destined no longer to be the only producer of modernity, to remain with the term we have already noted. This recognition leads to another. Consider Kant's thought once again. It is implicit that the Enlightenment contained the conclusion of the era of the West's primacy within it from the beginning. This should be taken positively. The Enlightenment was simply never Europe's possession—never the West's to disseminate. We find, at the end of it, that it has belonged to all of humanity all along. It happened for historical reasons to have emerged first in the West: This is the limit of what anyone can claim of it.

My years in Asia have been taxed again and again by the need to understand the challenges coming from the West. These essays reflect this preoccupation. But I end by rotating the gaze. The East has met its challenges, or is about to, or promises to, even if this outcome is sometimes distant. It is we Westerners who now face challenges. How shall we understand these? How shall we meet them? The act of tutoring requires a student, and we are losing the East as ours—if it has not, indeed, already graduated beyond our instruction. Who are we, then, in a century that does not belong to us?

NO ONE HAS BEEN more eloquent than Nietzsche in the matter of knowing ourselves. How shall we do this? he asks here and there all over his books. Reading back into our own past and considering it again—revaluation—was his answer. This required perspective—the gaining of a place from which we could see ourselves completely. This he called being "estranged from the present," an effect he urged us to pursue with purpose. Elsewhere he wrote of "questioning from behind" and "the perspective of the foreign." He wanted us to push off from our familiar shores, in one of his best-known metaphors. "Looking back at the coast from this distance we command a view, no doubt for the first time, of its total configuration, and when we approach it again we have the advantage of understanding it better as a whole than those who have never left it."

Nietzsche seems to have loved the thought. He saw Germany as a European, not as a German. Dilating the lens, Westerners would see life's fullness only when we saw with "an Asiatic eye." This Nietzsche expanded upon in one of his aphorisms: "Direct self-observation is not nearly sufficient for us to know ourselves . . . We have to *travel*, as the father of history, Herodotus, travelled, to other nations . . . to the so-called savage and semi-savage peoples, and especially to where man has taken off the garb of Europe or has not yet put it on."

Nietzsche wrote, not coincidentally, just as the West was colonizing the so-called savage and semi-savage peoples in the name of *la mission civilisatrice*. We can but marvel as to his ability to see forward. The West is now in more or less desperate need of a new perspective on itself. We must find it within ourselves to see with another eye. A revaluation of the values we live by—not least the notion of the West itself—is urgent.

It is often remarked that Asians know the West far better than Westerners know Asia. They have studied us, learned us, and then imagined themselves from our point of view. This has been a matter of historical circumstance: The modern era required it of them. Even today one finds again and again that the Chinese often draw their conclusions about China according to what Westerners think and say about China.

228 Somebody Else's Century

This latter, especially, is considered a peculiarity. I do not take it as such. These are natural reflections of the traveling Asians have done. They have, so to say, been through their Westernization and returned from it, ready at last to know and reclaim themselves. This is the importance of our moment. What are taken as Asia's peculiar habits, then, are a measure of the East's advance upon the West.

Much has begun to turn upside down as we progress into our post-Western era. In the nineteenth century it was to Asia's great disadvantage that it had to borrow so much from elsewhere and impose what it borrowed upon itself, with no connection to the root of what it borrowed. All that came had arisen and arrived from someone else's soil, and there was a strangeness about it. This strangeness is, in our time, another inversion, for it is among Asia's great advantages. It makes the East nimble in a way the West is not. All things and values can be changed, reshaped, made anew with an expedient agility, a detachment from the original, whereas in the West change must come slowly, for there is much to relinquish, a long past to the things and values that must be remade. Many train tracks must be pulled up before new tracks are put down. A strength in one century is a weakness in another, and vice versa. Time, self, nature: These were Asia's profound challenges as it encountered the West. Now its perspectives in these matters stand to be to its benefit.

We are accustomed to thinking of Asia's great borrowing from the West as among the historical oddities of our time. This is another misunderstanding. Borrowing is the very process by which cultures assemble themselves. All is fusion in the end. The line between East and West has been crossed as if it did not exist at least since the Greeks. Again, Asia comes out ahead in the twenty-first century in precisely the way it was behind in the nineteenth. It is now the West that must learn again to borrow and to ignore the imaginary line. The East can help us know ourselves if we learn to see with "an Asiatic eye." But we must learn the East, too. We must grasp its psychological complexity. This does not mean abandoning our own habits of mind. Emphatically it means understanding the limits of these habits and enlarging ourselves beyond them.

To change so as to remain the same, the Lampedusa thesis: This was Asia's strategy in the nineteenth century and all through the twentieth. Yet again there is a reversal, for Westerners must adopt it as their own now. The conditional nature of all values is part of the modern experience just as we ourselves shaped the modern. But the West is not so practiced at change as Asia, we find. And we come to yet another way to cast the matter of advantage and disadvantage. To remain the same, to remain unfertilized by others, is not among our alternatives. So we must reacquire our capacity to change, to learn from others, to borrow—the very thing the West once taught the East to do. And to do this, we must first board our boats, sail into the ocean, turn back from that desirable distance, and see ourselves altogether as we are.

AMERICA IS THE WORLD'S last eighteenth-century nation, the sole holdout in ours, the twenty-first. We are the last nation to cling to the old civilizing mission, the only ones left attempting to live by it.

Any detached review of events since the Cold War's end bears this out. We have cast ourselves in the recent past as "the sole superpower," or "the benevolent hegemon," or "the indispensable nation." What we have meant in these phrases, each less defensible than the one preceding it, has not been clear to us. We thought we were talking about our irresistible power when the true topic was our isolation as the world moved into the future. Without knowing it, then, we have acknowledged

that we stand alone as we uphold the values of the Enlightenment as they were originally understood. Nothing, we have
implicitly asserted, need change. Values formulated two centuries and more ago are perfectly valid as they are. In such
assertions no one, not even the English, has truly stood by us.

Europeans, I have thought, understood the ephemeral
nature of America's unchallenged power after the Berlin Wall
came down. They knew it was an interim destined to be brief.
More than this, it was with the dismantling of the wall that
Europe, without leaving the Enlightenment behind, revalued
it. This is how the late twentieth century is most plainly understood. For the Europeans there was to be no more emanation
of "progress" from one side of the planet to the other. To cast
the events of November 1989 in their simplest terms, the
human community had begun to erase the line between East
and West in the most literal fashion. This was history restarted,
not history at its end. It was just then that a "renaissance of
particularisms"—a good phrase from a good writer—appeared,
each representing a searching return to a buried past. This renaissance has sometimes arrived violently, but for its larger
meaning I have often taken it positively. If we had to choose a
moment when the post-Western era began, those dramatic
days and nights twenty-one autumns ago would be it.

Long before the Cold War's end, historians will eventually
conclude, Europeans had fundamentally lost what attenuated
taste for it they had had to begin with. We will understand,
soon enough, that the Atlantic world other than America
looked upon those decades as a kind of last stand for the
West, a final "mission." Europe was, truth to tell, fed up with
eighteenth-century projects. There is little exotic guesswork in
this. America's next mission, the "war on terror," has been a
failure on the world stage precisely because it came to no more
than a twenty-first-century rendition of the Enlightenment
narrative: the "we" and "they" of it, the "self" and the "other."

Any American who has traveled among others has heard certain things remarked upon again and again. Prominent among these is our capacity to alter course. "You Americans always change when faced with new circumstances"—this is a common observation. I have not found this to be so in the past several decades. Beginning in the late–Cold War period—roughly from the Reagan administration onward—the nation once justly noted for its capacity to change has been notable for its inability to change. We have instead been mesmerized by technological innovation and have mistaken the invention of new things for authentic change. They are not at all the same: The two, indeed, are not remotely related. No new device, with the possible exception of the atom bomb, has ever changed the way we think of ourselves in the world, and this is what needs to change—our values, our spirit.

Our preoccupation with material novelty, so oddly accompanied by a failure to achieve anything approaching genuine innovation, reached its zenith during the eight years of the administration of George W. Bush. That these years were a costly loss of time is hardly original to observe. It is now Americans who must reckon the price of a "lost decade." We measure this now in the distance that has arisen between America and the rest of the world—an Enlightenment nation and a post-Enlightenment planet. This was a period when our own erroneous distinction between spirit and things was at its most evident and contradictory. It was peculiar to watch, particularly from the East. The more Americans insisted on the efficacy of the American spirit, the more hollowly mythological it seemed, the more self-evident was our idolatry of technology, and the less one could deny the nihilism these habits masked. Great change amid no change, or no change amid great change: What we once observed among Asians we find in ourselves.

The election of Barack Obama in 2008 was a powerful moment in part because it suggested that Americans were at last prepared to consider their beliefs anew—to begin a revaluation of their own. This is how we should understand Obama's incessant emphasis on change. He means change of an authentic kind. This will involve taking from the eighteenth century all that is worth taking but living finally in the twenty-first. It will mean acquiring the capacity to see ourselves as being among others rather than apart from others. It will mean passing from Enlightenment to post-Enlightenment in our ways of thinking. This is the most accurate way of understanding Obama's purpose. It is a positive prospect.

As I complete these essays, the Obama administration is not quite one year old. Already one senses a decisive step has been taken, however difficult it may prove in practice to proceed. Already Americans seem no more likely to produce another George W. Bush than they are another Commodore Perry. Some turn in history has been made. There are grounds for optimism on this point. Even as resistance to Obama grows, we must insist that no outcome can be certain. Almost immediately, Obama reached across the imaginary line where it now matters most—between the West and the Islamic East. One senses post-Western thinking in such gestures.

WHEN THE REST of the world thinks of the West, we Westerners ought to ask ourselves, what is it they think of? Asians suggested an answer 150 years ago, and it is sobering to consider that it still applies. Faced with the West, others think primarily of science and method. Western values, as we think of them, have been less compelling than Western technology. All we have to offer, it would seem, are things.

One can debate just when the West became beside the point, so to say, but for its material accomplishments. Certainly this was so by the middle of the last century, the start of what we now call the independence era. But decolonization and its various outcomes may merely have underscored an established truth. Hans-Georg Gadamer, the celebrated German thinker, asserted thirty years ago that the West had been "provincialized" since 1914. "Only the natural sciences are able to call forth a quick international echo," as Gadamer gracefully put it. We must now include popular culture among the West's attractions. But this reflects no more than a taste for certain Western products—things, as against values or (in its true meaning) culture. As to when the West's provincialization began, why stop at 1914? Did Fukuzawa Yukichi and the Meiji oligarchs not make the point plain in the 1870s? The West was about "reason and number," we can recall. We were invited to keep the rest.

We must come to terms with the limit of what the world wants from us. It seems a paradox. As the Enlightenment recedes into history with its beginning, middle, and end all now visible, certain of its values prove universal. However many variations we may eventually count, the autonomy of the individual and his or her belonging in a democratic society are discoveries made in the West from which we can retreat no more than we can take back the invention of the compass. But others will find their way to the universal on their own, just as the West did. This is intrinsic to the very notion of values. What we call values are not, to put the point plainly, export items. The Enlightenment's influence looks to be eternal so far as we can grasp the idea of eternity. But it is no one's to send anywhere.

THE NINETEENTH CENTURY required many things of Asians. Fundamental among these, we have noted, was the reinvention of the self. The Asian self was divided into two with the arrival of the modern, the phenomenon we call doubling. The traditional Asian self, fluid and multiple, had one relationship with the past, the modern self another. The modern, Westernized self was superimposed upon the traditional, Eastern self.

Now we must consider the question from the opposite perspective. The nineteenth century prompted the construction of a Western self, too—the fixed, singular self of the nation-state. And as those years required Asians to make themselves over again so as to live amid the modern, Westerners are precisely so obliged now if we are to live in the arriving era. What, to put the question simply, have we made of ourselves? How shall we now remake ourselves?

This point will be difficult to grasp unless we sail far from our shores. The notion of the self involves the very frame of all our thinking. We have an idea of the self as stable and unchanging. How can it possibly be remade? And it is from within ourselves that we must think of and reconsider ourselves. This is the purpose of Nietzsche's "distance." And it is with distance that we discover how much that we presume is indelibly part of us—"who we are"—proves to be provisional. Asians have not yet fully resolved the question of self as it confronts them. How to belong remains one of the East's most fundamental conundrums, from Turkey and Iran all the way to Japan. This is a common enough observation, made in many different ways. But if we see ourselves with an "Asiatic eye," we will recognize that the questions of self and belonging are no more resolved in the West than in the East.

It is useful to recall two of the lines drawn earlier from Matthew Arnold:

Ah! Now 'tis changed. In conquering sunshine bright
The man of the bold West now comes array'd.

Who is this man of the West, we may ask, and how had he changed by 1867, when Arnold published these lines? Does Arnold mean what he seems to mean—the man of the West had been one thing and had become another?

We need look no further than Arnold's time. The nineteenth century transformed the Western personality. In "our century"

we set about defining others, and as we did so we defined ourselves. Arnold was drawing a picture of a new self in these lines.
The celebratory tone is unmistakable. The elements of surprise
and novelty are clear in the diction and vocabulary. Someone
new had appeared on the face of the earth.

Let us characterize this new someone. Arnold provides a useful frame. The self formed in the West during the nineteenth
century was bold, conquering, and altogether assertive—all
these being values identified with masculinity. This masculine
self was resolutely opposed to passivity or recessive habits. He
was radically individual and dedicated to action. Manifestation
was all; the hidden or unseen were of no consequence. Against
this we must consider all that the Western self was not—the
human qualities it denied itself. The new someone privileged
declarative individuality over embeddedness in a community.
He had no sensation of himself in nature. The present counted
for much, the past for little. He was able to see parts of things
but had little grasp of the whole. Reflection and intuition
counted not next to action. E. M. Forster wrote in "Notes on
the English Character" of "the undeveloped heart." It is a useful phrase. It tells us of a sensation of absence.

The self Arnold drew is the self we have inherited. Its values
are ours. But we tread the earth at a different moment. All that
the West was doing when Arnold wrote it is doing no longer.
We are called upon for different things now. Does it not follow
more or less inevitably that we must reconsider ourselves?
To think and act differently? To be other than who we have
become? Our utilitarian thinking, for instance: It is overripe
and so presents us not with a method of understanding but with
a limitation on our understanding. Life and experience, to put
it another way, exceed pure logic. Or our concept of the individual: This, too, is of another time and is unsuited to ours. A
post-Western world requires new thinking as to the meaning of
ego-centered subjectivity. We will not survive the Western

notion of the individual much longer. It must evolve—not all at once, as if by decree, but question by question, problem by problem, solution by solution. To put this simply, we must learn to live without "the West"—the West as an idea. It propelled us far, and for a long time. But now time is turning. This may seem a drastic notion. It may seem to suggest that we must alter our very relations with the world around us. Such is precisely the intended meaning.

Being of a utilitarian cast of mind, when we think of the East we think of its material rise. This is understandable, for economic power is what we can see, but it is logically indefensible. It is shortsighted in the extreme to imagine there would be no larger consequences in Asia's historic reemergence after its centuries in decline—that nothing will change other than the "Made in . . ." labels on the products we consume. Another consciousness, another way of looking at the world, is also reemerging. Discarding all notions of superiority and inferiority, we will be obliged to understand this. And then we will be obliged to accept its influence upon our world.

OUR MOMENT FINDS US adrift without our familiar boundaries. Those drawn on maps are intact, surely, but our imagined boundaries are disappearing in an inevitable erasure.

We should welcome our era's uncertainties, the not-knowing of how the post-Western story will come out. We stand to gain much as we dispense with our distinctions between human attributes as either "Western" or "Eastern." We will acquire the habit of seeing the whole, the continuity of things, rather than simply the parts, in Cartesian fashion. We will be able to make some use of "heterogeneous time" in our lives. We will see the past in the present, as opposed to our mental trick of placing it behind us, inaccessible and gone.

We are not so far from this as we may think. Let us not miss the extent to which we have already begun our travels. Much of what we are calling post-Western thinking is already within us. It exists in our midst the way the eccentric tradition arose in nineteenth-century England: It is what Indians call our alternative tradition, and it has long been there but marginal. The impulse to turn back, to reconsider our direction, extends back at least as far as Bacon and Descartes. Spinoza asserted persuasively that virtue and power are not, in the end, separable—a thought deserving of more consideration than we have come to assume. Some of our best thinkers have urged us for a century and more to overcome the tendency of science to fragment our perceptions and to connect what we habitually leave unconnected—one thing to another, the past to the present, ourselves to the natural world. Bergson, Heidegger, Sartre—they were all exposed to Eastern thinking and accepted its influence. So the turn in our own thinking concerns only prevalence. A post-Western world is one in which the previously marginal becomes something nearer to predominant—a part of mainstream thinking, in a phrase.

We cannot know our time so well as we know the past, for we are in and of the present. Perhaps there is some sense, even, to the Chinese practice of leaving the recording of one era to the people of the next. But to see as best we can is to recognize a moment of possibility, not of failure. The da Gama epoch draws to a close before our eyes—this is as good a characterization of our time as any. A case can be made that its true conclusion came in 1945 and that the Cold War simply prolonged it a final four and a half decades. Cast in this light, our "war on terror" is not so much a failure as a miscalculation as to where we are in history. And where we are in history is salutary: We have within our grasp the most momentous opportunity to advance the human cause since the Renaissance. The end of an epoch cannot be regretted once one recognizes the start of another.

ABOVE ALL, WE MUST resist the thought that a post-Western world somehow wishes to exclude us. This would produce in us our own versions of nostalgia and *ressentiment* and a kind of paranoia (at times already evident) about some imagined weakness. The case is quite the opposite. It is we who must surrender our exclusivity—our exceptionalism, in the American vocabulary. We can clash with other "civilizations," or we can converse. The invitation to the latter is extended; it is ours to accept or decline.

It is useful, perhaps, to think of a moment in Asian history long ago. This occurred in 938, when a general named Ngô Quyền defeated the troops of the Southern Han dynasty. A millennium of Chinese rule abruptly ended in what we now call Vietnam. Its new rulers then erected a court and a state modeled closely on China's. To reject another's tutelage is not to reject another's influence, or the imprint of history. Listen closely, and we find that this is what Asians have to say about the notion of "an Asian century." The thought itself is a figment in Western minds. It is much richer simply to conclude that the time to come is no longer ours the way another time once was.

I have often posed the question animating this last essay in exactly the terms I first related it. Can Asia recover its originality? Can it generate the substance of our world rather than accept it as others make it? Can it know itself apart from its great "other"? I have put this to many people in many places. The responses gathered in my notebooks are, predictably, nearly as varied. Most Chinese declare "Yes!" with alacrity. Most Indians shake their heads: Such a thing is an unrealizable dream. Elsewhere people are mixed on the matter, depending on belief, generation, and history. The Japanese tend to take the question away quietly for further consideration. These are no more or less useful than most generalizations.

My favorite reply by a long way came from an Indian friend in Ahmedabad, the city of Gandhi's great ashram, the commercial center of northwest India, a stop on the ancient route between East and West. Shiv Visvanathan, whom I have already mentioned, was a nimble thinker, thickset and possessed of a mischievous smile. We were finishing a long morning's exchange on the campus of his research institute, and we were to join others for lunch. The thread of our conversation would break.

"Shiv," I said, "let me put my question plainly. Are we witnesses to something new? Can Asians understand themselves without reference to the West?"

Shiv seemed to like the question. He grinned and missed not a beat.

"Why would we want to do a thing like that?"

Readings

Bergson, Henri. "The Perception of Change." Oxford, 1911. Reprinted in *The Creative Mind*. New York, 1946.

Chakrabarty, Dipesh. *Provincializing Europe*. Princeton, NJ, 2000.

Dallmayr, Fred R. *Twilight of Subjectivity*. Amherst, MA, 1981.

Gray, John. *Enlightenment's Wake*. London and New York, 1995.

Kant, Immanuel. *Foundations of the Metaphysics of Morals and What Is Enlightenment?* Indianapolis and New York, 1959.

Kapuściński, Ryszard. *The Other*. London, 2008.

Sarkar, Sumit. *Beyond Nationalist Frames*. New Delhi, 2002.

Sen, Amartya. *Identity and Violence*. New York, 2006.

An Acknowledgment

MANY FRIENDS, colleagues, acquaintances, and people encountered along the way helped in the making of this book—some for nearly thirty years, many more generously than one would have any right to ask. I cannot name them all. Each knows, I trust, that he or she belongs to this vast group and knows my gratitude to all in it.

Certain people had a direct hand. Carol Mann, my agent, asked two good questions and with them launched this project and changed my thinking as to what needed to be said in it. Dan Frank at Pantheon seems to be one of those editors who come along a few times in a generation: acute, intuitive, naturally gifted. With a courteously posed suggestion at the start, he altered the course more or less completely. The editing was of the same kind: thoughtful, never more than what was needed, always what was.

My readers did more than read. They also encouraged, cajoled, pushed, and pulled. Sara Vagliano of Stonington, Connecticut, cannot read a newspaper without a pencil in her hand, and from this habit I benefited greatly. Lynn Dennison of Kingston, New York, read, thought, critiqued, and then offered sanctuary when it was (so often) needed. Suzanne Lecht of Hanoi read the entire text and then answered incessant questions about it. To her, immense affection as well as gratitude.

A few others must be mentioned: Andrew Browne and his family in Beijing, the Mukerjee family of Calcutta, and Muriel Davis of New York. Each has had for me a givingness far beyond what we may ordinarily expect in our ungiving age, and each made much possible. I conclude this list with two people it is a special pleasure to name. Sheila and Chalmers Johnson were (once again) unsparing in their friendship, guidance, and support—all having arrived at a critical moment.

Three libraries were key. Staff at the Foreign Correspondents' Club in Tokyo, The University of Hong Kong, and the University Club in New York found, time and again, the apparently unfindable. Gratitude.

A brief note on translations, finally. I have altered the Sartre quotation at the start of the second essay from the published version slightly and strictly for the sake of grace. The translations from Renan that follow are mine and liberally rendered, but faithful to the meaning of the original lecture.